Intermediate PowerPoint 365

POWERPOINT 365 ESSENTIALS - BOOK 2

M.L. HUMPHREY

CONTENTS

Introduction

In *PowerPoint 365 for Beginners* we covered the basics of working in PowerPoint, including how to choose a design theme to work with, how to add, edit, and format text, and how to present or print your presentation.

This book continues from there and explores intermediate-level topics like how to add tables, images, and charts to a presentation. It will also cover how to work with SmartArt and Shapes. We'll also touch on some more obscure topics such as inserting 3D Models and Equations or creating sections in your presentation.

Note that I am writing this in October 2023 and that Office 365 is a constantly evolving product. So most of what I say here should remain relevant long-term, but I can't guarantee that they won't change the program in some way that means what I tell you here no longer works quite the same way.

At the end of this book we'll touch again on how to find additional help if you ever need it. As long as you know that something is possible, even if they change things slightly, you should still be able to do it with a little boost from the help function.

Okay, then. Let's get started with a recap of the terminology I'm going to use in this book.

Basic Terminology Recap

These definitions were already covered in *PowerPoint 365 for Beginners*, so I'm going to go through them fast. Even if you think you know them all, at least skim if you haven't read the beginner book because I may have my own quirks and you'll need to know them to understand the rest of the book.

Tab

I refer to the menu options at the top of your PowerPoint workspace as tabs. This is because in older versions of Office when you selected an option at the top of the screen, it looked like a file tab. In more recent versions of Office they've eliminated that appearance so that now the selected tab is simply underlined.

Examples of tabs are Home, File, Insert, Draw, etc.

Click

If I tell you to click on something, that means to move your cursor over to that option and then use the mouse or trackpad to either left- or right-click. If I don't say which, left-click.

Left-Click / Right-Click

Left-click simply means to use the left-hand button on your mouse or to press down on the left-hand side of your track pad. (For me on my track pad, it's the bottom of the track pad, but I think some have those buttons at the top instead.)

Right-click simply means to use the right-hand button on your mouse or to press down on the right-hand side of your track pad.

Left-Click and Drag

If I ever tell you to left-click and drag this just means to go to that selection, left-click and hold down that left-click while moving your mouse or cursor until you've selected all of the text, images, etc. or until you've moved that object where it needs to go.

Select or Highlight

Before you can make changes to your text, such as size, font, color, etc. you need to select the text you want to edit. If I ever tell you to select text, that means to go to one end of that text, and then left-click and drag to the other end so that the text is highlighted.

Another way to select text is to click at one end of the text you want to select, hold down the Shift key, and then use the arrow keys to select the text you want. You can also select separate sections of text by selecting the first one and then holding down the Ctrl key as you left-click and drag to select the next section of text.

To select an object, left-click on it. When an object is selected, there will be circles around the perimeter of the object.

To select more than one object, you can click on the first one and then hold down the Ctrl key as you click on the next one.

Ctrl + A can be used to Select All. If you are clicked into a specific text box and you use it, you will select all of the text in that text box. If you are not clicked into a specific text box, then Ctrl + A will select all of the objects on the page.

Dropdown Menu

Often there will be additional choices available if you right-click somewhere in PowerPoint. I refer to this additional set of options as a dropdown menu even though sometimes it will actually drop upwards instead of downwards.

You can also find dropdown menus in the options at the top of the workspace under the tabs where there's an arrow to the right or bottom of an option.

Expansion Arrow

Another way to see more options in that top menu is to click on the expansion arrows that are sometimes visible in the bottom right corner of various sections. Clicking on an expansion arrow will either open a dialogue box or a task pane.

Dialogue Box

The old-school way for Office programs to show you additional options was to use dialogue boxes which appear on top of the workspace. Some of the expansion arrows will open a dialogue box as will some of the dropdown menu options. You can see one if you right-click in the main space and choose Font from the dropdown menu or if you click on the expansion arrow in the Font section of the Home tab.

To close a dialogue box, click on the X in the top right corner.

Task Pane

In newer versions of Office, they tend to use what I refer to as task panes. These are separate work spaces that are visible to the sides or sometimes below your main work area.

You can close a temporary task pane by clicking on the X in the top right corner. You can also left-click and drag to undock a task pane and move it around. Or you can change the task pane's width by holding your mouse over the inner margin until you see an arrow that points left and right and then left-clicking and dragging to your desired width.

Mini Formatting Menu

If you right-click in the main workspace you will see at the top or bottom of the dropdown menu a mini formatting menu with the most common formatting options. This can be especially useful when working on a computer with a small screen where the menu options up top are not fully visible.

Scrollbar

To navigate between slides in a large presentation and through a long list of options in a dropdown menu, you will need to use the scrollbars. They run along the right-hand side or bottom of a given space when needed.

Control Shortcut

A control shortcut is when you hold down the Ctrl key (or sometimes another key) and then the specified letter to perform an action. So if I write Ctrl + C, that means hold down the Ctrl key and the C at the same time to copy something.

Undo/Redo

Ctrl + Z will undo the last thing you did. Ctrl + Y will redo the last thing you undid.

There is also a dropdown menu at the very top of the page with a backward-pointing arrow that will let you undo multiple steps at a time.

Slider

Some options in PowerPoint use a slider, which is a horizontal bar with a perpendicular line along the bar that marks the percent value currently being used. You can click along the slider or drag that perpendicular line to change the value.

Add Other Items to a Presentation Slide

In *PowerPoint 365 for Beginners* we focused on how to do a basic presentation that only used text. Now we get to cover the many, myriad other options you can add to a standard presentation slide.

If you look at a blank presentation slide that's been set up for it, you will see that there is usually a "Click To Add Text" note at the top of the main text box, but then somewhere below that text is a faded grid of icons. Like this:

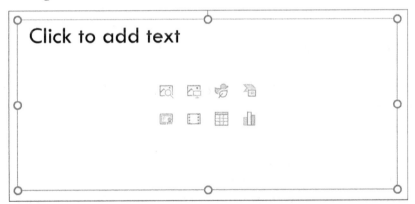

There are currently eight of these icons in my version of PowerPoint. They are, in order from top left and across and then bottom left and across, Stock Images, Pictures, Insert an Icon, Insert a SmartArt Graphic, Insert Cameo, Insert Video, Insert Table, and Insert Chart.

These icons may not stay the same and they may not stay in the same position. For example, in the two weeks since I wrote the first draft of this book and now when I'm editing it, they put Insert Cameo in there and removed Insert 3D Model. In the five years since I wrote the first PowerPoint guide, they've changed the order of these icons and increased the number from six to eight.

Good news is if you hold your mouse over each one it will tell you what it is.

Also, you can always use the options in the Insert tab to add any of these as well as a couple others:

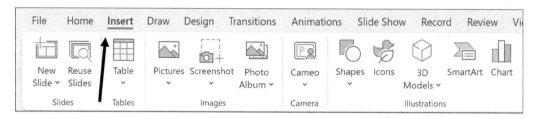

Stock Image is under the Pictures dropdown menu and Video is at the far end of the Insert tab, but you can see all the rest in the screenshot above as well as a few other choices like Shapes.

I am going to devote an entire chapter each to Tables, Pictures, Videos, SmartArt, Shapes, and Charts. But before we cover those I want to very briefly touch on Stock Images, Icons, 3D Models, and Cameos.

Stock Images

Click on the icon for Stock Images in a text box or click on the dropdown menu for Pictures in the Images section of the Insert tab and then choose Stock Images from there. Either way will bring up the Stock Images dialogue box.

By default it shows you a series of random stock photos, but there is also a search box you can use that will let you search for stock images by topic.

I'm not including a screenshot of that here because using stock photos can sometimes be an issue if you don't have the correct rights to use them. In general, stock is supposed to be safe, but it's always a good idea to read the fine print when using someone else's images. That's also why I'm not covering this topic in detail.

If you're just using stock images for a personal, small group presentation that won't be posted online, you're probably fine to use stock images.

If you're going to use them as part of an online course you sell or as part of a for-pay conference or in a YouTube video or something like that, you need to be more careful. That's commercial use and there may be limits you need to respect. Better to pay for your own stock photos off of a site like Shutterstock or Depositphotos and know exactly what your license allows, because the fines for misuse of a stock photo can be pretty steep.

Also, in this day and age, be very careful with any image that could be AI-generated since that hasn't shaken itself out at this point and most AI models were trained without permission on the copyrighted work of other artists. It's a possibility you could either lose any copyright you have in what you created if you use AI art as part of it, or that there could be a finding of damages at some point for people who used AI art without compensating the artists.

(If you're on the other side of that argument and think AI is great, don't reach out to me about it. Not interested in that conversation. Go find some online forum to be an AI champion. I'm just putting that caution out there.)

Anyway. To use stock images, find the image you want, click on it, and click on Insert. PowerPoint will then insert the image into your presentation. From there it will work just like a picture you insert, so see that chapter for those details.

Icons

PowerPoint also has a large number of icons that you can insert into your presentation. Either click on that Icons option in the text box or go to the Illustrations section of the Insert tab and click on Icons from there.

Both options will bring the Stock Images dialogue box up but it will be set to the Icons tab. You'll see a series of choices displayed and there will also be categories you can click on along the top as well as a search box. Find the icon you want, click on it, and choose Insert.

An icon is essentially a simplified line drawing of an object. If you want it to be a color other than black, you can insert it into your document and then go to the Graphics Styles section of the Graphics Format tab that will appear when you're clicked on the icon, and change the Graphics Fill color using the dropdown menu there.

Icons insert at a standard size but you can resize them by clicking and dragging on one of the white circles at the corner when the object is selected. (Don't drag from the sides because it will resize disproportionately and look weird.)

To move that object, left-click and drag when your cursor looks like arrows pointing in four directions which will generally be when you're near the perimeter of the object or on top of the illustrated portion.

3D Models

To insert a 3D model into your presentation slide, go to the Illustrations section of the Insert tab and click on the dropdown under 3D Models. This Device will let you find a 3D model you have saved on your computer. Stock 3D Models will let you use one of the Microsoft-provided models.

My cautions about using stock images apply to 3D models as well.

When you click on the 3D Models option for stock, you will see a dialogue box labeled Online 3D Models that has a series of categories to choose from as well as a search box. Mine right now is showing animated models, animated animals, animated for education, emoji, chemistry, anatomy, clothing, furniture, etc.

Click on the category and then select the model you want to insert and choose Insert.

I currently have an animated dog wagging its tail on my presentation slide. If you choose an animated option, you can click on pause in the bottom left corner of the text box that contains the 3D model to stop it from moving. Click on play to start it back up.

When the model is selected in your presentation there will be a circle with rotating lines up and down and then around in a circle that sort of reminds me of one of those atom drawings I saw back in chemistry class, but this one just has two sets of lines.

You can left-click on that and drag to rotate your 3D image.

For me, with the dog I chose, that's a little weird when I move it up or down. But side-to-side works well. With enough clicks and drags I now have a dog facing away from me and wagging its little tail at me.

These models are one of those things that can either be really useful or really distracting.

Cameos

Cameos are new for me, but since they chose to replace 3D Models with Cameos in that little list of choices, I feel I have to cover it to some extent. But if what I say doesn't make sense, then ignore it.

When I hold my mouse over Cameo in the Camera section of the Insert tab it tells me this is to "add your camera feed directly into your slides." You can choose to do this for this one slide or all slides from that dropdown. The icon that you can click on seems to match up to the one slide option.

Click on either the one slide option in the Insert tab or on the icon in your text box and it will fill that text box with an image of a stylized smiling person and open the Camera Format tab. By default, Preview is turned off. If you click on Preview in the left-hand side of that tab, you'll see whatever your computer camera shows.

So, if I'm understanding this correctly, it's a way to have yourself live on the slide as you present. A lot of video courses do this. Now it's an option built right into PowerPoint. As you might have noticed on my own videos that I've done for Excel, I don't do that personally. But you do you and now you can.

* * *

Okay. Now let's go in depth on the more common objects you might want to insert into a slide, starting with Tables.

Tables

To insert a table into a slide, the first option is to click on the icon for a table in an existing text frame. The icon currently looks like a three-by-three grid with a darker bar across the top. Or you can go to the Insert tab and click on Table from there. Here you can see both of the options:

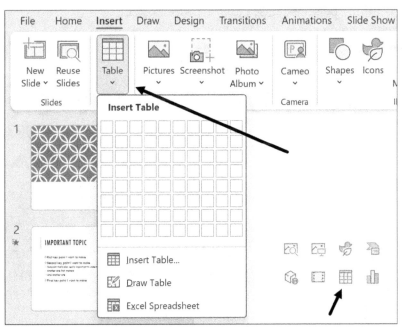

If you click on the table icon in a text frame, you'll see the Insert Table dialogue box which lets you specify a number of columns and rows to start with.

If you click on the Table option in the Insert tab, the dropdown menu will appear and you'll see a grid under the heading Insert Table.

Hold your mouse over any box in that grid and you'll see a table appear in the current slide that has that number of rows and columns. Also, the text above the grid will change to tell you the dimensions of the grid you're about to insert.

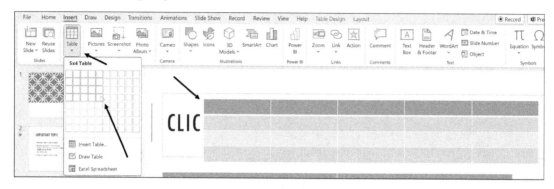

Click on that box in the grid to actually insert your table.

Another option is to click on Insert Table under that grid to bring up the Insert Table dialogue box.

You also can choose to Draw Table or insert an Excel Spreadsheet from that dropdown menu, although I don't personally use either of those often.

Don't worry too much about the number of rows, because those are easy to add. But do try to get the number of columns correct up front, it just makes life easier.

Okay then. Here I have inserted a 4 x 4 table into my slide:

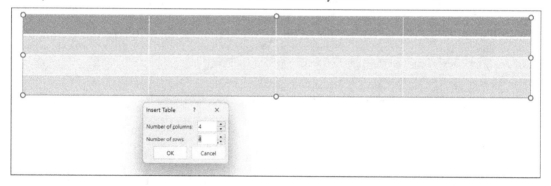

I also reopened the Insert Table dialogue box so you could see what that looks like.

From this point you just need to add your text and format the table. I usually add text first, but either way works.

Add Text

The easiest way to add text to a table is to click into one of the cells in the table and start typing.

To move to the next cell over, use the Tab key. If you need to go back one cell, use Shift + Tab.

If you use Tab at the end of a row, it will take you to the first cell of the next row. If you're in the last row of the table, it will add another row for you and take you to the first cell of that new row. If you didn't want that new row, the easiest fix is to use Ctrl + Z to undo.

Arrows do work in tables, but in different ways depending on where you are at the time you try to use them. Right and left arrows will move you to the next cell in that direction if you have no text in the current cell.

If you do have text in that cell then you need to be at the beginning of the text to move left one cell or at the end of the text to move right one cell. Otherwise the arrows will move you through the contents of the current cell one letter at a time.

Same with up and down arrows which will move you to the cell above or below if there's no text, but will move you up or down one row if there is.

(This is why I just tend to use the Tab keys or click into the cell I want.)

Usually in PowerPoint I enter my data directly into each cell. Somehow that's easiest for me.

But you can also paste in text from Word, Excel, another slide, etc. To do so, use Ctrl + C to copy your text from wherever it is, click into the cell where you want to place that text, and then either use Ctrl + V to paste or use one of the Paste Options available in the Clipboard section of the Home tab or by right-clicking on the cell in the table.

If the text you copy and paste is not already in a table format, then all of that text is going to paste directly into that one cell of your table.

If you select multiple cells before you paste, it will just paste that text multiple times, all of the text once per selected cell.

So if I have "test, test, test" on three separate lines in Word, and I paste those three lines of text into a table in PowerPoint, I will get a single cell in my table that has all three lines of text.

If you want what you paste into PowerPoint to paste into multiple cells instead, then you need to copy from a Word table or an Excel file that has the data separated already.

And you need to either click into the first cell where you want to paste your data or you need to select the correct number of cells in your PowerPoint table to correspond to the size of the source table.

If you select too many cells to paste into, PowerPoint will repeat your entries to fill the selected space.

If you don't select enough cells to paste into, PowerPoint will only paste in what fits into the cells you've selected.

The best way to see this is just try it. Write a few lines of text in Word and then try to paste them in, do the same with a few entries in different cells in Excel. And then try pasting them into a PowerPoint table with different numbers of cells selected each time.

Another thing to watch out for if you're pasting in values from elsewhere is that you may lose the text formatting in PowerPoint and have to fix that.

When dealing with numbers that have formatting, it can sometimes be much easier to do all of the calculations and formatting outside of PowerPoint and then just paste in the results. PowerPoint does have that Excel spreadsheet option, too, but for me when I just used it, the table it ended up inserting had zero formatting. I'd rather copy and paste from an Excel file and use the formatting that's already in a default table for a theme than try to use an Excel worksheet embedded in a presentation and have to do ALL the formatting to match the theme.

Which you prefer really comes down to where your strengths are. Excel is my #1 program so I'm far more comfortable there.

If you do want to use the insert Excel worksheet option in PowerPoint then let me give you a few tips.

First, when I click on that option it inserts a very small Excel window with only Cells A1 through B2 visible. To make that bigger and more workable, left-click and drag from a corner. Your cursor will be angled and have arrows at both ends when you're positioned to do that.

You can then enter data into those cells just like you would with a normal Excel spreadsheet. The menu tabs up top will show as Excel options while you have that open:

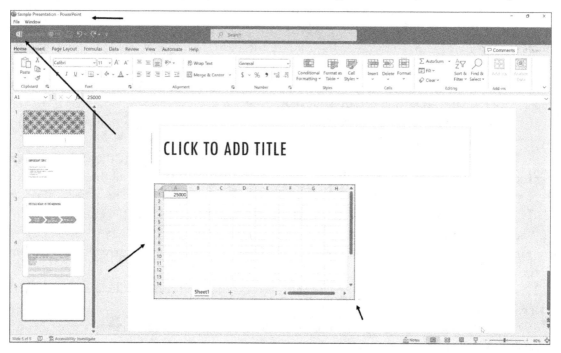

It's probably going to be a little hard to see in print, but at the top left corner right now I have the PowerPoint menu that still shows File and Window, but below that is all Excel. Those tabs for Home, Insert, Page Layout, etc. are the choices you see in Excel not PowerPoint.

So you can use any of those formatting or other options up there just like you would in Excel.

When you're done entering data, click away from that box and you'll have a table where the number of columns and rows matches however many rows and columns you made visible when you expanded your table:

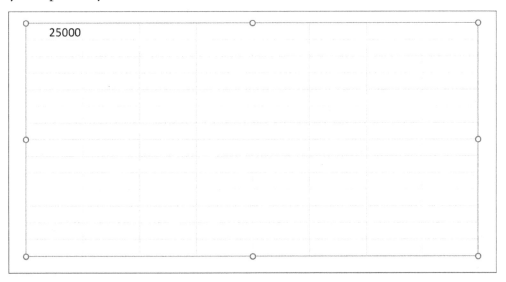

See what I mean by lack of formatting? And PowerPoint treats this as a shape not a table so you need to go back into Excel to format the table.

To do so, double-click on that image to open it back up as an Excel worksheet. You can then use the Excel options to format the table. Any formatting you do when it's open as an Excel worksheet will remain when you click away again:

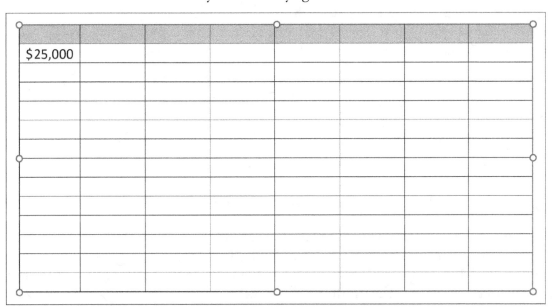

Here I added some shading in the first row, added borders around all cells and formatted the currency entry. But I also had to be careful to constrain my Excel view to just the cells I wanted to include on the slide.

It's...eh. It helps with number formatting or formulas, but it's a little fiddly to work with. So, enough of that. Let's pretend that you're just going to work with a basic table in PowerPoint instead.

When you insert a table and are clicked onto that table, there are going to be two new menu tabs available to you, Table Design and Layout:

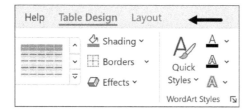

Table Design lets you make your table pretty or fancy by choosing different colors, border styles, etc. Layout lets you control the more basic format of the table including number and size of rows and columns.

Let's start with the options available under Layout. I'll also mention as we go along other ways to make these changes.

Layout Options

It's very rare to have a table where all of the columns are the same width and all of the rows are the exact same height, so chances are you'll want to make some adjustments like that for any table you insert. Most of those options can be found on the Layout tab:

Let's walk through them now.

Column Width

To change the width of a column in a table, you have a few options.

The easiest, to me, is to hold the cursor over the edge of the column until the cursor looks like two parallel perpendicular lines with arrows pointing to each side. Left-click and drag the column border until the column is the width you want.

The total width of the table will not change, which means the neighboring column you drag towards or away from is going to also adjust in width to maintain the total width of the table.

Here you can see that I made Column 1 skinnier and this had the impact of making Column 2 wider. (I started with all columns the same width as Column 3):

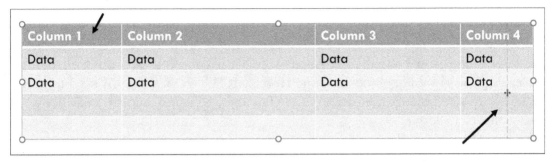

You can also see that I'm in the process of changing the width of Column 4—see the dotted line and the cursor that looks like those two parallel perpendicular lines with arrows pointing left and right.

With that Column 4, because it's the edge of the table, changing that column width from the edge will also change the overall width of the table.

(This example used those two parallel lines with arrows pointing to either side, but actually the easiest way to click and drag from the outer edges of a table to change a column width, is to go to the white circle along that edge and left-click and drag while the cursor looks like a white arrow pointing left and right.)

You can see the white circles along the edge of the table above. They're generally at the middle of each edge and the corners.

Another option for changing your Column Width is to click on a cell in the column you want to change, go to the Cell Size section of the Layout tab, and change the Width value there:

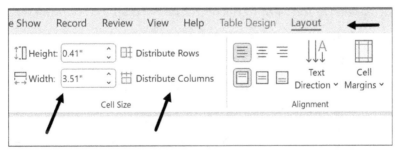

If you want all of your columns to have the same width, click into the table and then click on the Distribute Columns option in the Cell Size section of the Layout tab. The table width will not change, but all of your columns will adjust so that they are equal widths.

Row Height

Adjusting your row height works much the same way as adjusting your column width, with one small exception. Your row height is always going to automatically change to at a minimum fit the contents of your cells. You cannot have hidden text in a table in PowerPoint.

How this works is if you try to set your row height to a very small value, the row height will automatically change to a height that can still display all of the text from the cells in that row.

If there is no text in a row, the row height will stay tall enough to fit one row of text in the font size shown in the Font section of the Home tab. Which means you'd need to select all cells in that row and change the font size for all of them to a small enough value if you want to make that row shorter.

So.

Option one for changing the row height is to position the cursor over the top or bottom border for that row, and then left-click and drag to the size you want.

Option two is to go to the Cell Size section of the Layout tab and change the Height value for that row that you're clicked into.

And, technically, a third option for changing row height is to change the font size for all of the cells in that row when that row has no text in it.

To make all of your rows the same height, click into the table and use the Distribute Rows option from the Cell Size section of the Layout tab.

Changing the height of a single row does not impact the height of the row above or below it. But it will change the overall height of the table.

Keep in mind as you add text to a cell in your table, your row height will change to accommodate that text. This is why I usually save setting my column widths and row heights for the end after I have all of my text in. It lets me decide whether I'd rather make a column a little bit wider to get all of the text on one or two rows, or whether I'm fine with a row that is taller than the surrounding rows because the text in that cell wrapped around to a new line. I can also decide to change font size to make things fit better at that point.

Insert Columns

To insert an additional column into your table, click into a cell next to where you want to insert the column, and then go to the Rows & Columns section of the Layout tab and choose either Insert Left or Insert Right, as appropriate.

The overall width of your table will remain unchanged, so inserting a column will impact the width of all of the other columns in your table. This is why I try to get the number of columns right from the start. Less formatting hassle.

The width of the inserted column is generally going to be the same as the width of the column that you were clicked into when you chose to insert it, but both will have proportionately adjust to accommodate that new column.

So, for example, right now I inserted a column into a table while clicked into a column that was 2.33 inches wide. My new column is the same width as the old column, but they are both now 1.86 inches wide because every column in the table had to shrink some to fit that new column.

You can also click into a cell, right-click, and choose Insert Left or Insert Right from the mini formatting menu if those choices are available. That menu is dynamic, so they may not be.

Insert Rows

The easiest way to insert a new row at the bottom of your table is to just go to the end of the far right cell in the last row and use the Tab key.

You can also click into a cell in the table where you want the new row to be inserted, and then go to the Rows & Columns section of the Layout tab, and choose Insert Above or Insert Below. The row that is inserted will be the same height as the *default* height of the row you were clicked into.

Inserting a new row will change the overall height of the table. No other row heights will be affected but watch that the new row doesn't take your table off the page. (If it does, try making the table wider to fit more text on a line or change your font size to fit more text. You can't click and drag from the corner to adjust it.)

Delete Columns or Rows

To delete a column or row, you can select the entire row or column and then use the Backspace key. (Using the Delete key will remove any text but leave the actual column or row in place.)

Your other option is to click into a cell in that row or column, go to the Rows & Columns section of the Layout tab, and then click on the dropdown under Delete and choose to Delete Columns or Delete Rows from there.

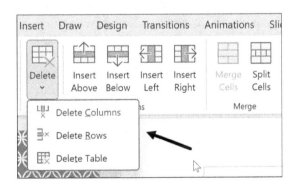

Delete Table

To delete an entire table, you can use the Delete Table option in that Delete dropdown in the Rows & Columns section of the Layout tab which we just saw.

Or you can select the whole table when your cursor looks like four arrows pointing left and right and up and down, and then use either the Backspace or Delete key.

Select Table

I usually select a table by using the cursor when it's pointing in all four directions, but sometimes that's annoying to get working. It usually requires putting your cursor somewhere along the outer edge of the table.

Another option is to click anywhere on the table, go to the Layout tab, and then use the dropdown under Select in the Table section on the far left to Select Table.

With either of those options it won't look like anything happened, but if you use Backspace or Delete the table will be deleted.

Select Row or Column

I usually just left-click and drag to select all of the cells in a row or column.

But you can also click into a cell in the table that's in that row or column, and then go to the Table section of the Layout tab, and choose Select Column or Select Row from the Select dropdown menu.

Selected cells will be grayed out in comparison to other cells in the table.

Merge or Split Cells

It is possible to merge or split selected cells within a table. I always save this for as long as I can if I'm going to do it, because it makes the rest of your formatting more difficult to do.

Here is an example of a table that uses this sort of formatting:

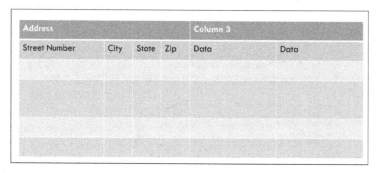

Note how the number of columns differs across rows? The first row only has two columns. The second row and all those after it have six columns.

A table like this can either be built from merging cells, so in this case I'd start with six columns and then merge the cells in that first row. Or it can be built my splitting cells, so in this case I'd start with two columns and then break those up into four columns and two columns, respectively, for the rest of the rows.

In a table like this, if you add a new row it will have the same number of columns as the row you were clicked into when you added the new row. So once this is set up I can go to the very bottom cell of that table, use Tab, and have another row with six columns in it.

To merge cells together, select the cells you want to merge, go to the Merge section of the Layout tab, and click on Merge Cells. The selected cells will all become one cell and any text in those cells will be brought into that one cell starting with the top left cell, going across that row, and then left to right for any additional rows of cells that were merged.

And, yes, you can merge across columns and down rows at once.

Another way to merge cells is to right-click after selecting your cells and choose Merge Cells from the dropdown menu.

Split Cells works in a similar way. Select the cells you want to split and then either right-click and choose Split Cells or choose Split Cells from the Merge section of the Layout tab.

Split Cells can be applied to a single cell, but usually I want it for a range of cells in one column.

Both split cell options will bring up the Split Cells dialogue box. It has fields for the number of columns and number of rows you want your selection split into.

Each selected cell will be split according to your choice. So don't enter the total number of columns and rows you want to end up with. That's not how it works. If you have four cells selected and you choose two columns in the Split Cells dialogue box, you will end up with eight columns. Four cells, each split in two.

Which means if you work with Split Cells sometimes it takes a little math or experimentation to get the appearance you want. And sometimes it's better to just select one column or one row and work from that or to merge everything and then split it if you don't have content in those cells yet.

One final note, when you split cells, the text stays in the top left-most cell of the group created out of that cell. So if I split a single cell into three rows and three columns, the text will be in the top left cell and the other eight cells I created will be empty. If I did that to two cells at once, each grouping of nine cells would have the text that was there before for that cell in the top leftmost cell of each cluster of nine.

It may sound confusing. It is a bit. If you need to do this, experiment and remember that Ctrl + Z, Undo, is your friend.

Text Alignment

As with most table designs, you may decide that you don't want your text in the default position, which is left-aligned and top aligned. Often, for example, for columns with numbers that are providing a count of entries, I will center the values. For currency values, I may prefer to right-align.

You have nine total alignment choices because there are three choices about how you align text left to right and three choices about how you align text top to bottom. (We'll cover text direction, which is another choice, next.)

Here is a table with nine cells in it that uses each combination:

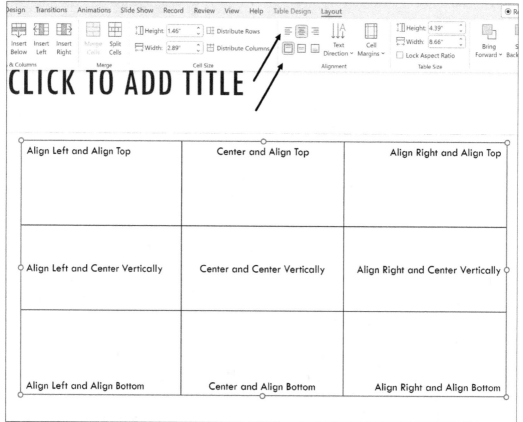

The alignment options that I used are available in the Alignment section of the Layout tab. The top row of choices gives you Align Left, Center, and Align Right. In the row below that you can choose from Align Top, Center Vertically, and Align Bottom. Each option shows text that is aligned in that manner.

The screenshot above has Center and Align Top selected. They have light gray boxes around them to show that they're the current selections.

Sometimes you won't see the difference between two choices, because the column is too narrow or the row height is too short to show the difference. That's why I always wait to make this choice until I've added all of my text and finalized my column widths and row heights.

The left, center, and right options should always be available in the mini formatting menu. Top, center, and bottom may or may not be available.

To apply alignment, just select your cells and then make your choice.

Text Direction

With all of those choices we just walked through, the text was still left-to-right. It was just a matter of changing where it fell within that cell.

But you can also change the direction of the text in a cell. Those options can be found under the Text Direction dropdown menu in the Alignment section of the Layout Tab. Here we go:

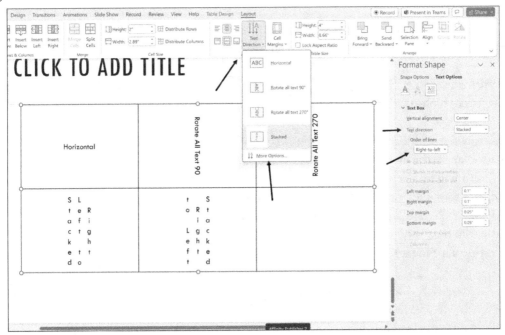

There is a More Options choice at the bottom of that text direction dropdown. Clicking on it will bring up the Format Shape task pane on the right-hand side of your workspace which you can see above. The Text Direction dropdown menu there has the same four choices.

Horizontal is the top left example in that table there. It's the default. The next cell in that table shows the rotate all text ninety degrees option. The next cell shows the rotate two hundred and seventy degree option.

Your final option is Stacked. You can see examples in the bottom row of the table above.

Stacked puts the letters one on top of each other from top to bottom until it reaches the bottom of the cell and then it starts a new column. Note that it will start a new column mid-word, so you need to pay attention when using it.

The default is stacked left-to-right but in the Format Shape pane you can choose right-to-left instead.

For me, personally, I use Horizontal primarily but will sometimes use Rotate All Text 270 if I have merged cells along the left-hand edge of a table.

Cell Margins

For the most part, you should be able to leave this setting alone. It can be found in the Alignment section of the Layout tab. The dropdown menu for Cell Margins will show four options or you can choose to customize your settings.

Use cell margins in situations where your text is going too close to the edge of the cell or not close enough.

Table Size

You can manually set the size of your table in the Table Size section of the Layout tab. By default, though, you will be constrained by the contents of the table, especially when setting your height value.

The way around this is to check the box for Lock Aspect Ratio first. If you do that, then you can change the height to a smaller value than the contents would normally allow, and PowerPoint will adjust the font size to make that work.

You can also click on a table and then click and drag from one of the white circles around the edges to change a table size, but the Layout menu option with Lock Aspect Ratio is probably the best way to do this.

The Format Shape task pane also has a setting for table size.

Table Design Options

Now let's turn our attention to the Table Design tab where you can make your table look pretty.

Table Styles

Table Styles are pre-formatted options for your table design. There are seven different color options:

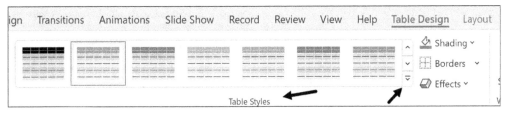

Click on the downward-pointing arrow on the bottom right of that section (noted in the screenshot above) and you'll see that there are a lot of styles to choose from within each color group:

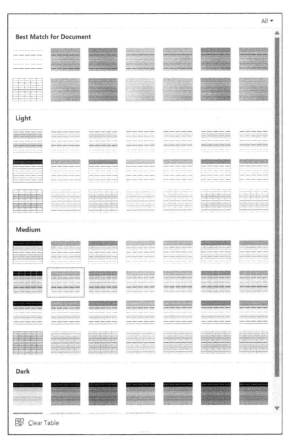

Across each row the design is the same, but down each column is a different color.

In this presentation theme, the left column is black/white/gray and but the other columns use blues or greens. The colors here will vary depending on presentation theme.

The options are split between Best Match for Document, Light, Medium, and Dark. Personally, I think that "Best Match for Document" category does not show a very good understanding of what I'm doing, but honestly, the category names really don't matter. Just find the one that looks the most like what you want.

You can hold your mouse over each of the options to see it applied to your table. Click if you want to keep it.

I do think it's best to add text to the table first before doing this. Of course, for me these styles are never quite what I'm looking for, but they can be a good place to start.

Table Style Options

Once you get close to what you want, you can then customize from there using the checkboxes in the Table Style Options section:

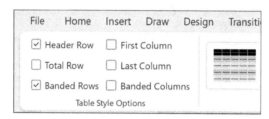

You can see that right now the Header Row and Banded Row options are checked for my table. And this is what that looks like:

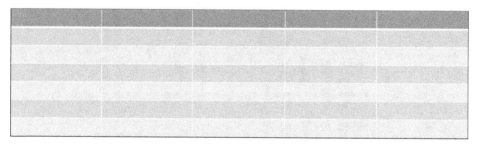

Note two things. The first row of this table is a different color. That's what happens when the Header Row box is checked.

Second, the remaining rows in the table alternate between two colors, one darker and one lighter. That's Banded Rows.

If I want to turn both of those off and not have them in my table, I can just uncheck those boxes. And here we go:

Pretty ugly, huh?

What about the other choices there? Total Row will make the last row of the table a different color. First Column will make the first column of the table a different color. Last Column, you guessed it, makes the last column a different color. Here are all three applied at once:

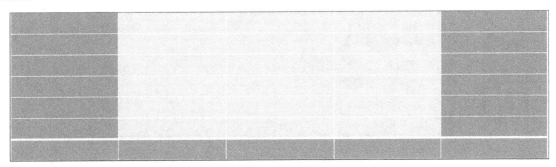

Doesn't really work, does it?

Note, too, that for the Total Row the border directly above that row is slightly thicker. The same thing happens for the Header Row where the border below is slightly thicker.

Finally, there is an option for Banded Columns that does for columns what Banded Rows does for rows. It makes every other main body column a different color.

I would recommend not having banded rows and columns together, because that creates a checkerboard appearance in every other column which looks weird.

The point of banded rows and columns is to let you scan over or down more easily. So if your user is going to primarily be reading across the table, use banded rows. If they're going to be primarily reading down a column in the table, use banded columns. For smaller tables you may not need either one.

And again, I'd recommend having your text in your table first before you make these choices.

Shading

You can also manually apply your own color to cells in the table using the Shading option. To do so select the cells you want to change, and then go to the Shading dropdown menu in the Table Styles section of the Table Design tab:

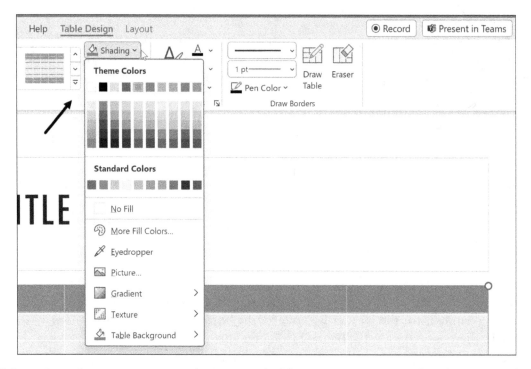

Click on the color you want to apply. You can hold your mouse over each color to see what it will look like before you make your choice.

To stay compatible with your template, it's best to keep within those first seventy color options which will be customized to the template.

But you can also choose one of the Standard Colors, or click on More Fill Colors to bring up the Colors dialogue box which lets you specify a custom color or choose from pretty much any color that exists.

There are some other options in that dropdown like Picture, Gradient, and Texture that we're not going to cover here in detail. They do exist if you really want to go there, I'd just remind you that your presentation exists to support what you're saying not to steal the show from you.

That dropdown is also where you can choose No Fill to remove a color from your selected cells.

And there's an Eyedropper option there that will let you choose a color from another element in your presentation.

Borders

By default, your theme will probably already use some sort of border. In this example that I've been working with, the borders are white and go around every cell by default. But you can change that.

Select the cells where you want to apply your borders and then use the dropdown for Borders in the Table Styles section of the Table Design tab to select the type of border you want:

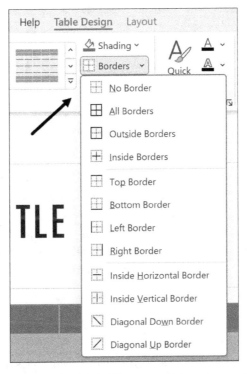

Now, there's a 50/50 chance that you didn't like something about the border you just applied. Chances are it's because of the color of the line or the width of the line.

To fix that, you need to Undo and then go to the Draw Borders section of the Table Design tab. In that section you can change the type of line, the width (point size) of the line, or the color (pen color) of the line:

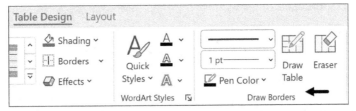

Nothing will change after you make your choices until you then go back and apply the border to those cells again. You can click on each line you want to change while your cursor looks like a little pen or you can use Esc to turn that off and then select your range of cells to format and use the Borders dropdown menu once more.

Here I changed my line color and width and then used the All Borders option on every cell in my table:

I think I'd need to see data in there to see if it works, but you get the idea. I'd probably ultimately keep that thicker blue border around the perimeter and the top and bottom rows but go with something more subtle for the data rows in the interior.

Sometimes when working with borders it takes a few different tries or multiple applications of borders to get the look you want. I often like to have a thicker outer border around a table and then a thinner border around the cells in the table itself, for example, which requires application of two different sets of borders to the same cells.

Effects

No.

You can see below the Borders dropdown in the Table Styles section of the Table Design tab that there is an option for Effects. This lets you apply bevels, shadows, and reflections to cells in your table or your entire table. Maybe don't?

I mean, I'm sure there's a reason this menu exists. I think it's more useful when working with WordArt or Shapes, though. So I'm just going to tell you not to do it. But if you want to do it, select your cells, go to the option you want, hold your mouse over each one to see what it will look like, and then click to apply.

WordArt Quick Styles

Same with WordArt. You could apply it to the text in your table. I'm sure there have been times when someone did and it worked. But for your standard business presentation? Eh. I'd say leave it alone. Better used on the first page of a presentation or in the title field. Or for when you're creating something like a book cover in PowerPoint. (Although there are better programs for that and some are even free. Email me if you need recommendations.)

Again, though, if you want it, select the text in your table you want to apply it to, hold your mouse over the options under the Quick Styles dropdown to see what your text will look like, and then click to apply. To customize your appearance, use the Text Fill, Text Outline, and Text Effects dropdowns next to that.

Font Color

There is one useful option in that WordArt Styles section of the Table Design tab, and that's the top dropdown there for Text Fill. Choosing a color from that dropdown should change the font color of your selected text.

Personally, I use the Font Color option in the Font section of the Home tab instead, because I am a creature of habit. The mini formatting menu will also work. As will right-clicking, choosing Font from the dropdown menu, and changing the Font Color in the Font dialogue box.

Draw Table

The Draw Table option in the Draw Borders section of the Table Design tab is another way to split columns or rows. It was a little temperamental for me, but I was able to get it to work.

Make sure your line type, width, and color are what you want before you start, and then click on Draw Table. Your cursor should look like a pen.

Left-click somewhere within the cell where you want to draw a new border, but not on the edges of the cell. Hold that left-click and drag to draw a line. That should split that cell into either two columns or two rows depending on the line you drew.

You can only split a row if it's tall enough to accommodate two lines of text already.

Be careful, because if you click and drag from the edge of a cell instead, it will draw a new table on top of your existing table that's one cell wide by one cell tall.

As long as your cursor looks like a pen, you can keep drawing lines. Click on Draw Table again if it turns itself off.

When you're done, use Esc to turn the tool off.

Eraser

The Eraser tool, which is also in the Draw Borders section of the Table Design tab, lets you remove lines from a table. Click on it and then click directly on the line you want to take away.

You may be left with a black line around the perimeter if you erase a perimeter line, but that's just there to indicate the boundaries of your table. If you bring up the presentation slide you'll see that there's actually no line in that spot on the presentation.

Be careful with this one, because I was able to create a scenario where it removed the line between two cells so they appeared as if they were one column, but they remained two separate cells. But in other examples I was able to erase the line and have it act like I'd merged those cells. So test your result.

Use Esc to turn it off when you're done.

Move Table

You will probably find that sometimes you accidentally move the table around when what you really wanted was to change a column width or row height. Ctrl + Z to Undo is probably the best choice in those instances. But, if you want to manually change the location of a table, either Select the table or click onto the table when the cursor is a four-sided black arrow, and then left-click and drag the table to where you need it.

To center your table on the slide, you can click on the table and then use the Align dropdown menu in the Arrange section of the Layout tab. Choose Align Center to align it left-to-right or Align Middle to align it top-to-bottom.

Keep in mind with Align Middle that you may have a title section on your slide and PowerPoint will not take that into account. By default it is going to align to the overall slide. So manually positioning the table may work better in that scenario.

Pictures

Next up is inserting pictures. In a text box you will usually have an icon for Stock Images and one for Pictures. Pictures is for when you're using an image from your own collection.

The Images section of the Insert tab also has a Pictures option where you can choose between This Device, Stock Images, and Online Pictures.

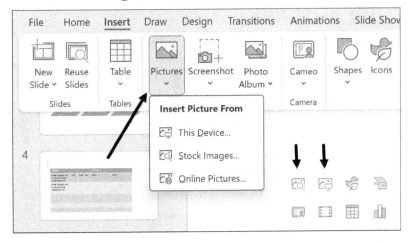

This chapter is for Pictures from This Device. I already mentioned Stock Images and the risks around using those. Copyright applies to all images you didn't take yourself, so be aware of those restrictions. I have a lot of photos I have paid to use over time, but even though they are on my device I still need to know which ones I'm allowed to use when. There are often limits on how long you can wait before you use an image and/or on how many copies of a product can be sold before that license becomes invalid.

Insert

Okay, lecture over. Click on This Device or the Picture icon in your text box. Either one will open the Insert Picture dialogue box.

Navigate to the image you want to use, click on it, and then click on Insert.

That Insert option has a dropdown that will let you choose to Link to File or Insert and Link instead. This can be useful if you have images that might get updated later and you want the presentation to automatically update.

But there are risks there, too. If you choose Link to File and you move that file or try to open the presentation on another computer that can't link to that file, you won't have that image in your presentation. It will be a blank box with an error message in it.

When I inserted my image into my presentation slide, PowerPoint brought up the Designer task pane on the right-hand side with all sorts of formatting suggestions for the slide:

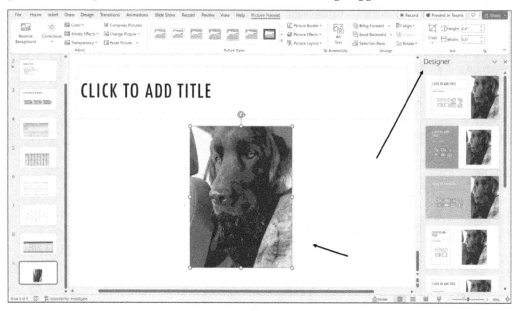

You can see the slide as it is now in the center. It just has my image (of my dog who I loved very much) with a title field above. Pretty boring and basic.

On that right-hand side the Designer is showing layouts that use that image and have a title section but also have another text box where I could put more content.

If you like one of those layouts, click on it to use it.

Another thing to note here, my photo adjusted to fit that text box. It's at 47% of its actual size right now.

Also, the text box changed size to match my photo's dimensions. By default, any photo you bring into a text box will either be fit to the height or width of the box, in this case the height, and then the other dimension will adjust so that the box is exactly the size of the picture.

When you're clicked onto an image inserted into your presentation, you will see a Picture Format tab with a number of adjustment options. Here you can see the left-hand set of choices:

Here are the right-hand set of options:

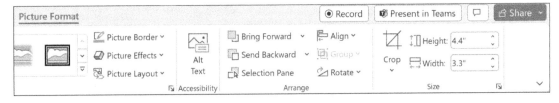

Let's now walk through what you can do with these.

Resize

The easiest way to change the size of a picture is to left-click and drag from the corner of the image. By default the image will scale up or scale down as you drag, keeping the height and width proportionate. So if you just want to eyeball your measurements, that's the way to go.

But sometimes you want all of your images to be an exact height or an exact width. When that's the case, click on the image and then go to the Size section of the Picture Format tab and change the Height or Width value there by clicking into one of those two boxes and typing the value you want.

By default that will also scale proportionately. (Which is generally what you want, because if you don't scale proportionately your image distorts and doesn't look like it should.)

You can use the expansion arrow in that Size section to open the Format Picture task pane and then uncheck Lock Aspect Ratio if you don't want that.

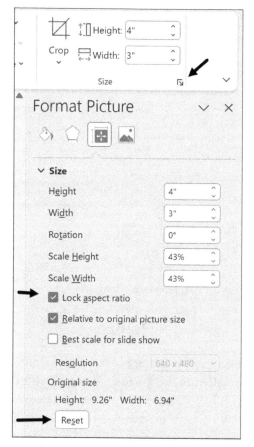

The Format Picture task pane also has a Reset option that will change the image back to its original size. Not the size it originally came into PowerPoint, but its original size before you imported it. For me with this image, that would be 9.26 inches by 6.94 inches which is too big for the slide.

Best Scale for Slide Show, which is another option, was also a bad idea in my case.

Move

Sometimes when you rescale an image, it moves around a bit. When that happens you will want to move the image back into place. The easiest way to do this is to left-click on the image when your cursor looks like a four-sided black arrow and then drag the image back into place.

As you left-click and drag the image around, look for very faint dotted lines that will appear as you align with different elements on the slide. For example, with a slide that has a title text frame it shows me when the image is aligned to the left edge, the center, and the right edge of that text frame as well as the top edge, middle, and bottom edge.

If you still have your Format Picture task frame open, you can also expand the Position section under Size & Properties and specify an exact position relative to the top left corner or the center of the slide. (This can be useful if you have images in the same exact position on consecutive slides and you want them to be in exactly the same spot on each slide.)

Another option is the Align dropdown menu in the Arrange section of the Picture Format tab. Choose the alignment you want from there.

Alt Text

For a presentation that you are giving to an audience, you probably won't need alt text. But if you're doing a PowerPoint presentation that is going to be circulated to others and watched online, then it may be useful to use.

PowerPoint makes an attempt to add alt text when an image is imported. If you ever need to see and/or edit that text, right-click on the image and choose View Alt Text from the dropdown menu.

This opens a task pane for Alt Text on the right-hand side of your workspace:

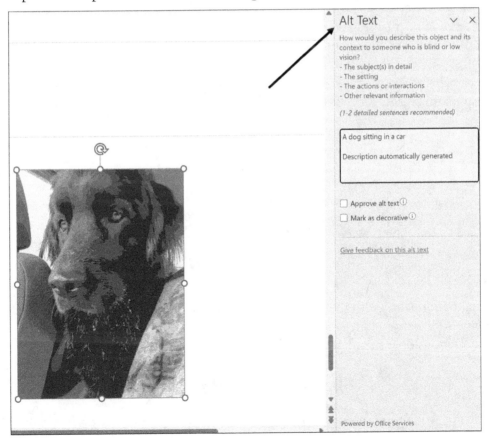

You can see here that it described my image as "A dog sitting in a car" which is accurate. Now, if I'd been using this image to demonstrate how to posterize an image, I might want to change that to something like "Posterized image of dog sitting in car". Or if I'd been demonstrating something about black dogs, I might need to add that it's a black dog. Or a Newfoundland. What Alt Text you put depends on the reason for using the image.

You can see here that it also included a note that this was an automatically generated description which tells a user it may not be a good description for purposes of this presentation. You can approve that alt text by checking the approval box below the description. Or you can edit the text by clicking into the text box and making changes. If the image you imported is just there for decoration and doesn't need to be described, click the Mark As Decorative box.

Rotate

Sometimes a picture comes in sideways or maybe you want to rotate it for other reasons.

One way to do this is to go to the Format Picture task pane and enter a value for Rotation in the Size & Properties section. It's the third choice under Size.

That lets you be precise. You can enter 90 or 270 to rotate the image right or left by ninety degrees. If you already rotated the image and want it back to where it started, change the value to zero.

You can also rotate the image directly on your slide. There is a little looping arrow usually at the top of the image. Just left-click on that and drag:

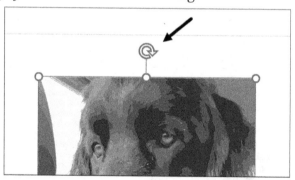

Your final option is to go to the Arrange section of the Picture Format tab and click on the dropdown for Rotate and then choose to Rotate Right 90 or Rotate Left 90. Clicking on More Rotation Options opens the Format Picture task pane.

Flip Vertical or Horizontal

You probably won't need this one, but if you ever do, under that Rotate option in the Arrange section of the Picture Format tab there are two other choices, Flip Vertical and Flip Horizontal:

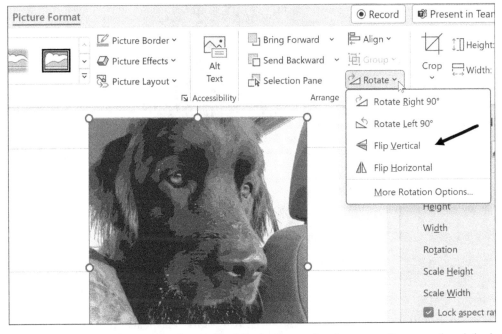

Here, I have flipped the image horizontally. Notice how the dog now faces to the right instead of the left. If I were to flip vertically the dog's head would be at the bottom of the image.

Be careful if you flip an image that there isn't text in the image because the text will be backwards or upside down.

Crop

Sometimes you bring in a picture and don't want all of the image. To fix that you can crop your image. The option is available in the Size section of the Picture Format tab. Click on Crop or in the dropdown menu there choose Crop.

That will place black markers at the corners and around the edge of your image. Left-click and drag on any of those black lines to crop from that spot inward.

Here you can see the grayed out area that will disappear if I accept the cropping I've done so far:

You won't see the black bars as you're dragging, they only reappear when you're done moving that black line.

You can crop more than one side at a time. Do the first one, let up on your left-click and then left-click and drag on the next bar.

When you're done, use Enter or Esc or click away to lock in your cropped image:

For any image that isn't fully visible on your slide, you can click on it, choose the Crop option, and then left-click and drag the image around to change what part of the image will be visible. You'll see the visible part in color and the parts that won't be visible grayed out.

Once you have the image positioned the way you want, click away, Esc, or Enter.

Note that there were other crop options in that dropdown like crop to shape that we're not going to cover here but that you can use to have your image appear in a star or circle or some other shape.

Another way to bring up the Crop option is to right-click and choose Crop from the mini formatting menu at the bottom of the dropdown menu.

Align

As we discussed with tables, there are also alignment options for pictures. You can align a picture to the left, center, right, top, middle, or bottom of the slide using the Align dropdown menu in the Arrange section of the Picture Format tab.

You can also align objects to one another.

I will sometimes if I have three or more pictures in a slide, select all of them and then use the Distribute Horizontally or Distribute Vertically options. This makes the space between the images equal and is easier than trying to do it manually.

It's also possible with multiple images to align them left, center, right, etc. to one another instead of to the slide. You just need to select them and, if it doesn't happen automatically, change the Align to Slide option at the bottom of the dropdown over to Align Selected Objects. After that you can choose the type of alignment you want. When you do this, the objects will align within the space created by their outermost edges. That means that sometimes to get the look I want I have to move the outermost object outward or inward to create the correct perimeter for PowerPoint to align within.

Bring Forward/Send Backward

You probably will not need this for most presentations. But if you ever have images or elements on the page that overlap one another, you can bring an element forward so that it's on top or send one backward so that it's underneath any other element.

To do so, click on that element and then go to the Arrange section of the Picture Format tab and choose Bring Forward or Send Backward. Those choices work to bring the element one layer forward or send it one layer backward.

In the dropdown choices for each, you also have the option to Bring to Front or Send to Back. That will place the element either all the way at the front or all the way at the back.

This really only comes into play when you have multiple overlapping elements, though. If everything is in its own space, no need to worry about this.

Picture Adjustments

PowerPoint has a number of options for image adjustments. For a standard presentation I don't expect you to need these so I'm going to run through them fast.

On the far left there is an option for Remove Background. If you click on that, it gives you a pen that you can use to select the parts of the image that you want to keep or another one for selecting areas to get rid of. I've had to use tools like this with book cover design projects and I have to say it's pretty decent. In about thirty seconds I was able to do this:

See how all the blanket and seat sections of the image are now gone but you can still see the individual hairs on her ears? Not bad.

So if there's something in your image that you don't want there, this may be the way to fix it.

Next to that is the Corrections dropdown menu:

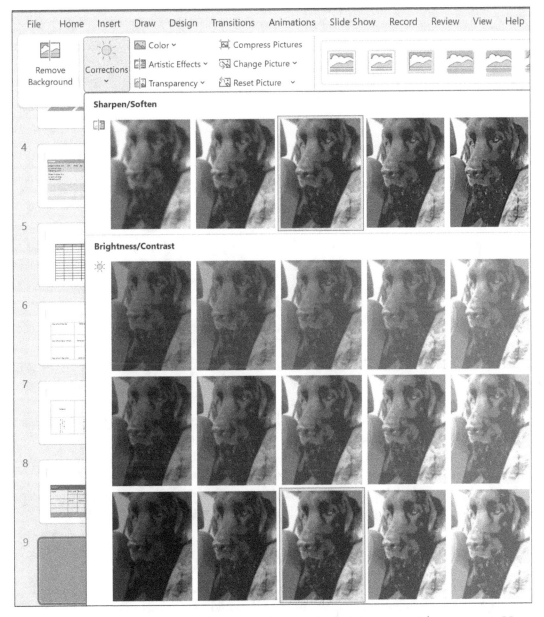

This lets you sharpen or soften an image or change the brightness and/or contrast. You can see what each one will look like in that dropdown. Just click on the one you want.

If you need more control, click on Picture Corrections Options at the very bottom and that will open the Format Picture task pane to the Picture Corrections options, which includes sliders for Sharpness, Brightness, and Contrast.

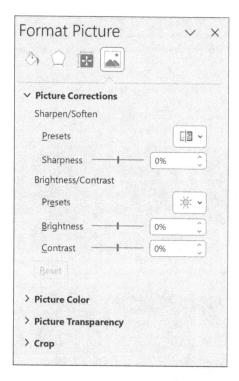

Next you have dropdowns for Color, Artistic Effects, and Transparency. Each dropdown has thumbnails of the image and what it will look like under each setting. Click on the one you want.

In the bottom of the next column of choices is an option to Reset Picture which lets you either reset the picture adjustments or, if you use the dropdown, reset the picture and its size. Just keep in mind that if you reset size you take the image back to its original size, which for me in this presentation was too large an image.

The Change Picture option there lets you choose a new picture to replace the current one. If you do so you will lose any adjustments you had made to the original picture.

Picture Styles

After the Adjust section in the Picture Format tab is the Picture Styles section. I generally don't use this much for business presentations, but I could see someone using it. There is a dropdown menu there with pre-formatted choices that let you apply frames or effects around your picture:

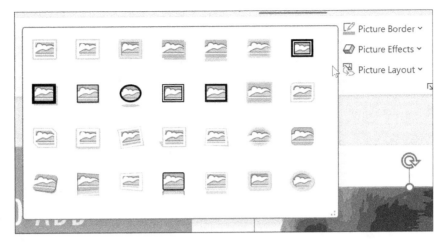

Off to the right side of those choices there are dropdowns for choosing a picture border or picture effects. You can refine a pre-formatted style using those options or create something from scratch.

Here I used the double frame option in the pre-formatted styles section but then I changed the border color over to match the slide:

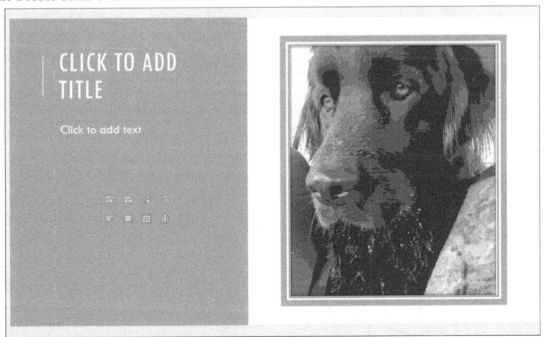

Plenty of options to play with. Just, once again, remember that the purpose of the presentation slides is to help you convey your message so don't let all the bells and whistles take over from what you're trying to do.

Picture Layout

There is a dropdown for Picture Layout in the Picture Styles section of the Picture Format tab. Ignore this one. It's for SmartArt which we'll cover shortly.

Videos

Now let's talk videos. I have seen many a presentation that had a video embedded. To do so, you can either click on the Insert Video option in a text box, which currently looks like a snippet of film, or you can go to the Insert tab and choose Video from the Media section at the far right of the Insert tab.

The dropdown options in the Insert tab are This Device, Stock Videos, and Online Videos.

For Online Videos, PowerPoint currently supports YouTube, SlideShare, Vimeo, Stream, and Flip. If you use online videos you are subject to each provider's terms of use and privacy policy, so be sure you know what you're doing. But you just give the address of the video and go from there.

If you use the Insert Video option from the text box on a slide the default is to find a video on your device.

I think most people who use videos will be pulling videos from somewhere like YouTube, so let's do that. First, go find the video you want to use. I have some Excel videos up on YouTube so I'm going to use one of those.

Once you find the video, copy the website address.

Next, go to the Insert tab and choose the Online Videos option from the dropdown menu for Video in the Media section. Paste in your address. It will show you a preview of the video:

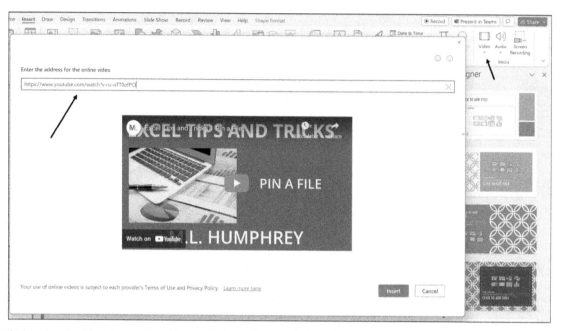

If that looks like the right video, click on Insert. The video will show on the slide with a big play button on it:

For me that inserted image looks pretty blurry, but when the video plays on the slide it looks okay.

If you instead insert a video from your own device, it will come up with the play bar below the image, like so:

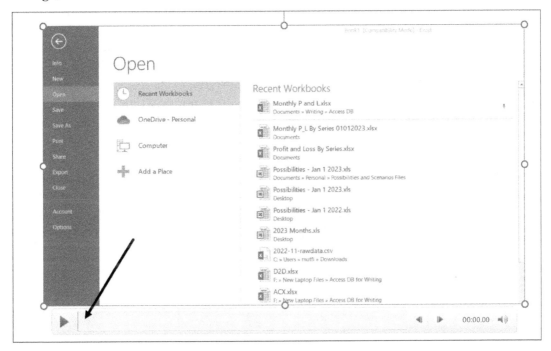

That's not the best thumbnail image it's showing, but it is the image that starts that video because this was the original video without any bells and whistles like a title image added. So keep that in mind if you use one of your own videos. Make sure the video has a good starting image.

Anyway. For either one, you just click the black triangle, wherever it is on the page, to play your video. During a live presentation you may need to hold your mouse over the video image to see it.

There are a number of options for formatting or editing a video after you insert it. Those options are available under the Video Format and Playback tabs that appear when the video is selected.

Video Format has Adjust and Video Styles sections that let you change the brightness or color of the video as well as apply poster frames or a shape to the video. There are also Accessibility (Alt Text), Arrange, and Size options that are similar to what we saw with Pictures.

The Playback tab really only works for your own videos. It has options that let you bookmark a section of the video, add a fade in or out, trim the video, or choose how the video is played or displayed. These options are largely grayed out if you insert a YouTube video, though, and I expect it's the same for other outside videos.

I'm not going to do a deep dive on videos, but a few points.

If you add a bookmark, that just lets you click to that point, it doesn't start the video at that point. For that you should probably trim the video.

You can set a video to play fullscreen.

You can also set a video to loop until stopped. This is a good way, for example, to have images that display on the screen while you're waiting to start your presentation. Make a simple little video with images of your company or your topic and set it to play until stopped.

If you want captions on your video, the format they need to be in is WebVTT. You'll have to upload that file separately. (You could also just generate a version of your video that has your captions embedded so that you don't have to go through this, but the drawback to that is they may overlap content in the video and can't be turned off. Most online platforms don't allow that type of video.)

You can choose when the video should start playing. Choices are automatically, when clicked on, or in click sequence.

And that's pretty much it. The big work on videos happens before you embed them most times. Once they're properly created, it really is usually just a matter of find it, embed it, and click to play.

SmartArt

Okay. Time to talk about one of my least favorite topics in PowerPoint but one that is used very often, especially in consulting contexts: SmartArt.

Theoretically, SmartArt is great. It lets you create these complex flow charts or diagrams that really illustrate what you're trying to say.

The reason I don't like SmartArt is because of how much I've seen it misused or abused. So, please, for the love of all that's holy, think when you use SmartArt.

Do these items belong together? Is this the right image to portray this relationship? What information do you need to include to show the relationship and what can be removed?

Really make sure that what you're doing makes sense. Because if it doesn't, you lose your audience. There is someone like me sitting there no longer listening to you because I don't understand why that pyramid has three completely unrelated items in it.

Rant over. Now let's walk through how to use this.

Insert

To insert SmartArt into your slide, either click on the Insert a SmartArt Graphic option from a text box, or click where you want to place it and then go to the Illustrations section of the Insert tab and click on SmartArt from there.

Both options will bring up the Choose a SmartArt Graphic dialogue box:

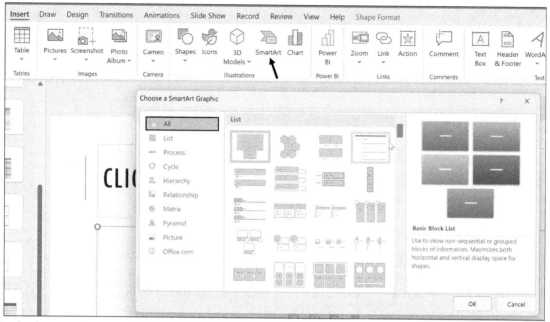

In the image above it is showing the Basic Block List. Note how there is a description on the right-hand side related to how to use this image. It says this image is for non-sequential or grouped blocks of information. So you wouldn't use this one for a process flow.

On the left-hand side of the dialogue box are categories of types of image. So if I have a product life cycle I want to illustrate, I could click on Cycle and see my choices:

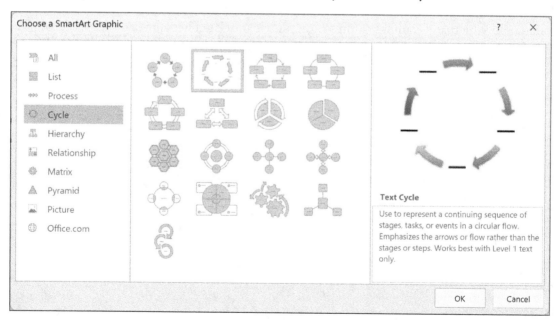

Here I've clicked on Text Cycle which it says should be used to represent a continuing sequence. It also says it works best with Level 1 text only, which means that you could have a label for each arrow, but wouldn't include subpoints or further details.

So the first step is to find the SmartArt that works for the information you want to present. Once you've done that and clicked on that option, click on OK to insert it into your slide. I'm going to go ahead and choose Basic Chevron Process. Here is what I get:

You can't see this in print, but the colors used for the graphic match my presentation theme. Now we do all the work of adding and formatting this so it works for our purposes.

Add Text

The next step is to add text to the graphic.

When I inserted the graphic, PowerPoint automatically opened the SmartArt Design tab for me. In the top left corner of that tab there is an option for Text Pane. When I click on that, I get this Type Your Text Here dialogue box:

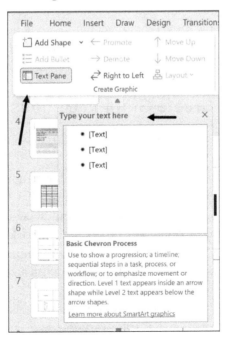

I can click into that dialogue box and replace those [Text] entries for each bullet point with my own text. Each bullet represents an element in the SmartArt, in this case a chevron.

If I need more elements than the three it started me with, I just use the enter key to add another bullet point.

As I add additional bullet points in the Text Pane, PowerPoint adds an element to the graphic and resizes all of the elements so they still fit on the slide. It also adjusts the font size so that the text fits on each element. Like so:

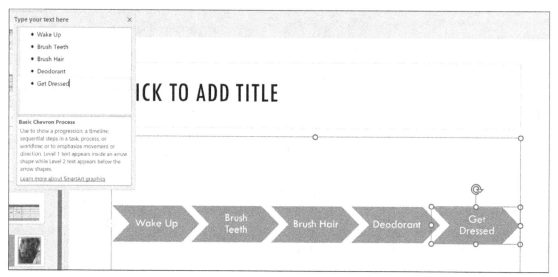

See how I have five chevrons now instead of three, but they still fit in the same space left-to-right.

You can also click directly onto an element and edit the text that way. That's often the easier choice if you just need to fix a typo or add/delete text from one element.

Create Graphic Options

In that same Create Graphic section of the SmartArt Design tab are some other options for customizing your SmartArt.

Add Shape will add another of that shape into the illustration.

Add Bullet will, in this case at least, add a bullet point *below* the selected design element.

Demote will remove an element from the graphic and make it into a bullet point below the graphic. Promote will take a bullet point from the slide and make it an element in the graphic.

Right to Left will change the direction the arrows are pointing in your graphic. The name of this one doesn't change depending on which direction the arrows are pointing, so just think of it as "change direction".

(By the way, this last week I saw a presentation that used a circular flow and did it counter-clockwise and my first thought was that the presenter had chosen chaos. This is probably cultural, but the default directions for information flow in the U.S. are going to be clockwise, left-to-right, and top-to-bottom.)

Move Up and Move Down move the selected element one spot up/left or one spot right/down in the SmartArt graphic.

Layouts

Next to the Create Graphic section in the SmartArt Design tab is the Layouts section. This section has a number of choices for that type of SmartArt. So here, for example, are various process layouts:

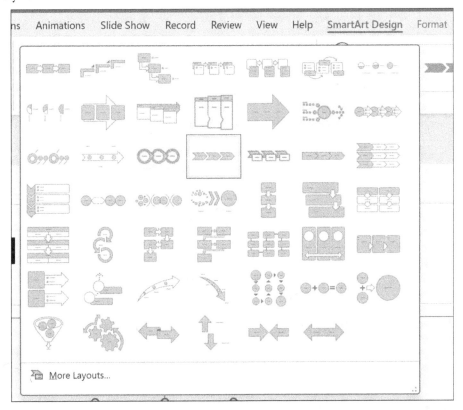

(By default you'll only see that top row of choices. Click on the downward-pointing arrow with a line in the bottom right corner to expand to see all choices like I did above.)

Here I changed the image over to another of the layout choices, but it still works because they're both process illustrations:

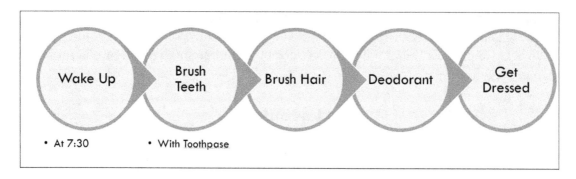

Change Colors

The next option in the SmartArt Design tab is the Change Colors dropdown menu in the SmartArt Styles section. If you don't like the color that PowerPoint chose for your SmartArt, you can change it here. Hold your mouse over each option to see it temporarily applied to your SmartArt and then click on the one you want.

Each Accent category is one color. Across the row for that accent category are the various format choices:

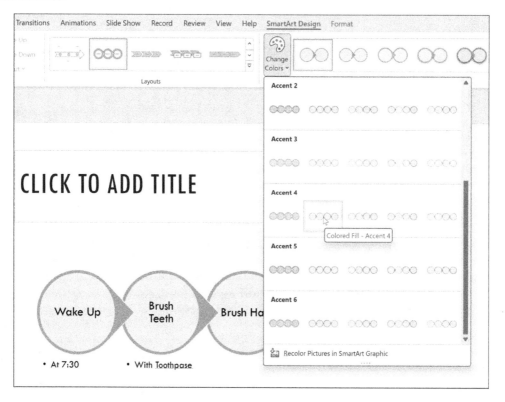

SmartArt Styles

The Change Colors option lets you change colors and style at the same time, but if those style options aren't quite what you want, there may be other choices available that work better in the SmartArt Styles section set of choices:

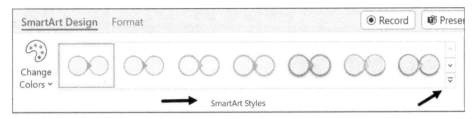

Once more you can click on the downward-pointing arrow with a line in the bottom right corner to see more choices. Or you can just arrow down to see one row of choices at a time.

For this specific layout the choices are pretty limited, honestly, but you can try them. Hold your mouse over each one to see what it will look like, click if you find one you want to use.

Reset Graphic

The Reset Graphic option in the Reset section of the SmartArt Design tab lets you take the SmartArt back to what it looked like before you did any special change of colors or SmartArt Styles. It retains the number of elements and text that you added, though.

Convert

The Convert option in the Reset section of the SmartArt Design tab lets you convert your SmartArt graphic to text or shapes.

For shapes it looks the same at first glance, but it's no longer SmartArt. Now it's just a series of shapes that you can still edit, but maybe not as easily. You can tell this by looking at the tab options up top which will have a Shape Format tab when you click on the image but no SmartArt Design and Layout tabs anymore.

For text it turns it into a bulleted list and removes all the images.

It is possible to take a bulleted list like this one above and convert it to SmartArt. Just select the text (Ctrl + A), right-click, choose Convert to SmartArt from the dropdown menu, and then choose the graphic you want to use:

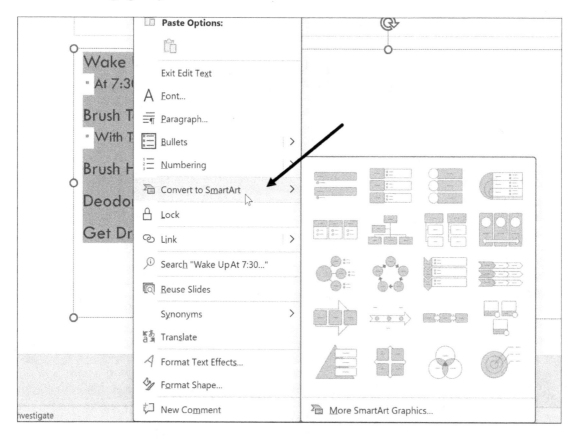

Format Elements and Text

The Format tab that appears for SmartArt is for changing the color, shapes, and effects for the elements in your SmartArt. It should look familiar by now because it's basically the same as for other items you can insert into a presentation slide.

To format your SmartArt, click on an element(s) and then you can apply whatever formatting you want to that element. (Use Ctrl + A to select all of the elements at once or use Shift or Ctrl as you click on each element you want to include.)

The default colors you see under the various options should be colors that are compatible with your presentation theme. So if you stick to those top 70 color swatches, especially if you stay within one row or one column, the elements in your SmartArt should work well visually with the rest of the elements in your presentation.

Depending on the element you have in your SmartArt, the Shape Fill and Shape Outline options may not do exactly what you want them to do. Same with the Change Shape option.

So if you want to make those sorts of changes, you may be better off working from the SmartArt Design tab and choosing a different layout instead. But you can experiment and see what's possible. Just remember that if something doesn't work Ctrl + Z, Undo, is your best friend because it's often easier to back away from a bad choice than try to move forward and fix it.

Okay. On to Shapes.

Shapes

You can add pretty much any shape you want to a PowerPoint slide. The other day I had to draw money flows for someone who had five bank accounts and ten places that money came from and another ten places the money went. None of the SmartArt was going to do that well. So I just created it from scratch using shapes.

I don't want to bog down in this too much, but I do want to at least cover the basics for you.

For me, working with shapes, I want a completely blank slide to work with. So if I have a template that has a title field and text field for the default slide, I add a new slide and then delete both.

To delete any element on a slide, click on it until you see the white circles around the perimeter, make sure you're not clicked into the box where you can add text, and then use Delete or Backspace.

Insert Shape

To insert a shape, go to the Insert tab and click on the dropdown under Shapes in the Illustrations section:

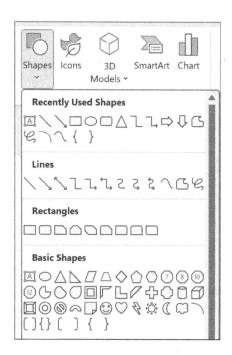

Click on the shape you want.

(There are even more choices that you can't see here, this is just the top of the dropdown menu. But it gives you a good feel for what you can add to your presentation slide.)

A few key shapes to discuss.

Text Box

That first option you can see there under Recently Used Shapes that has an A in a box and that's also visible in the Basic Shapes section, is the text box option.

If you want to add text, you need to use a text box.

Click on that option and then left-click and drag on your presentation slide to create your text box. There will be a cursor in the box, start typing to add your text.

By default, the height of the text box will match the text you enter into it. So it really doesn't matter how tall you make it to start, it's going to shrink down to your text. You can fix this after you add the text box by changing the height value in the Size section of the Shape Format tab.

Arrowed Lines

In the Lines section you can see a variety of line types. If you want to point from one spot to another, be sure to choose a line that has an arrow at one end (or both if that's what you need).

If you need a line that has a bend in it, choose the ones that show that in their thumbnail because a straight line can't be bent later

It works the same as a text box, click on your choice, and then left-click and drag on your slide to place the arrow where you need it.

For curved or bent lines, you can adjust the bend later by clicking on the line and then left-clicking and dragging the circles on the lines to change the shape. That's also how you can change the length or position of the endpoints for a straight line.

To move a line, left-click and drag the line while your cursor looks like arrows pointing in all four directions.

Other Shapes

There are obviously a lot of other shapes you can choose from in that dropdown menu. For each one, click on your choice in the Insert Shapes dropdown menu. For most you then left-click and drag to create the shape on the slide. For the scribble option, you left-click and drag to draw.

Once a shape is inserted into your slide its shape and dimensions can be changed by left-clicking on the image and then left-clicking and dragging the circles that appear along the lines that form the image. The only exception, I believe, is the scribble option which is set in the form you created, but can be resized like a photo by clicking and dragging from the edges.

Shape Styles

For every shape you add, there will be a Shape Format tab available when you are clicked onto that shape.

That tab has sections for Shape Styles and WordArt Styles. For the most part, you should already know how those work. For lines use the Shape Outline dropdown or Shape Styles options. For two-dimensional shapes use Shape Fill, Shape Outline, and the Shape Styles options.

Arrange Shapes

When adding a bunch of shapes to a slide you may find that some are on top of others and that you don't like one blocking out the other but you want both in that position. Or maybe you have three shapes on the slide and they don't quite line up visually even though you want them to.

The Arrange section of the Shape Format tab is where you need to go to fix those sorts of issues.

We already discussed a bit the Bring Forward/Send Backward options. Those are how you put one element in the foreground or move it to the background so that any element it overlaps is hidden behind it or shows on top of it.

Selection Pane will open the Selection task pane to let you see all of the elements on that slide. You can then lock an element so it can't be changed by clicking on the padlock shape or you can hide an element by clicking on the circle with a line arcing over the top:

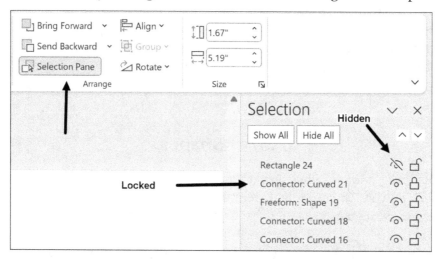

Here for Connector: Curved 21 I've locked that shape and for Rectangle 24 I've hidden it. The other elements on the page are still capable of being seen and moved around.

In this case, it was easier to lock that one element and then go back to the slide and use Ctrl + A to select all of the other elements and align them to one another than it would have been to try to individually select each one.

With respect to aligning elements on the slide, if you select one element the default is to Align to Slide. If you select more than one element the default is to Align Selected Objects.

When you Align Selected Objects they align within the space covered by those elements. So imagine drawing a rectangle around the selected elements based on where their edges fall. That's the space PowerPoint will use for alignment.

With multiple elements selected, you can choose to Align to Slide also, you just need to make that choice in the dropdown menu after you've selected those elements, and then reopen the dropdown menu to make your alignment decision.

You can also group elements using the Group dropdown in the Arrange section of the Shape Format tab. If you group elements together they act as if they are one element. So if I want a colored circle with text on it, I'd put in a shape for that circle and then a text box and I'd align the text box over the circle and then group the two together so that I can then move them together without worrying about them becoming misaligned. They'll also show as grouped in the Selection task pane.

Once you've grouped elements, you can use that same dropdown menu to ungroup them.

Charts

Okay, time to talk about charts.

Insert

You can insert a chart by clicking on the icon for Insert Chart in a presentation slide text box or by going to the Insert tab and choosing Chart from the Illustrations section.

What you will see with both choices is an Insert Chart dialogue box. Here you can see both options as well as the dialogue box:

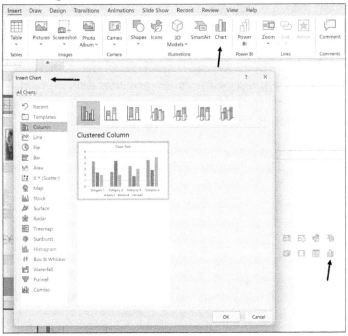

I am not going to cover here the uses for the various types of charts. If you want to learn that, look to my Excel books where I do discuss how a column chart differs from a line chart and from a pie chart, etc. For this book, I'm going to assume you know what you're doing.

Click on the chart type you want and then click on OK.

PowerPoint will insert into your presentation slide a pre-populated chart that has fake data in it:

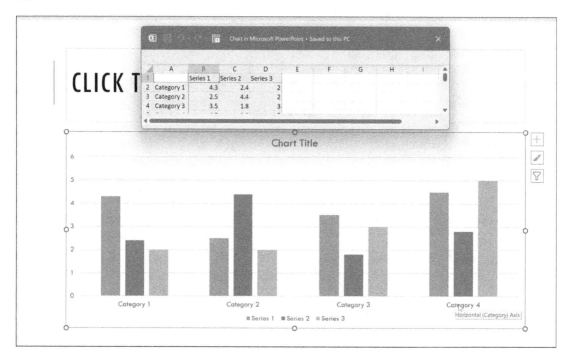

You can left-click and drag from the bottom corner of that Excel spreadsheet to see all of the data fields. Click into the Excel spreadsheet and enter your values to replace the fake ones. As you update the data, the chart on the presentation slide will also update:

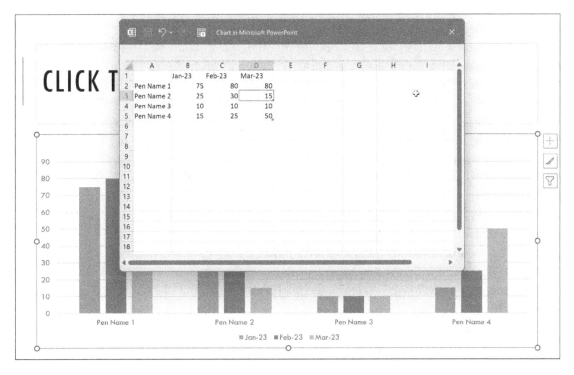

When you're done inputting your data, click the X in the top right corner of the Excel spreadsheet.

Edit Data

If you ever need to edit your data again, right-click on the chart, and choose Edit Data from the dropdown menu to bring up the Excel file again.

You can also go to the Chart Design tab and click on the Edit Data option in the Data section there.

Edit Appearance

The colors used in your chart should by default work with your chosen presentation theme but there may be other edits you want to make.

To edit the appearance of your chart, it works much the same way as it does in Excel so I'm going to cover this quickly. When you click on your chart, there will be a Chart Design tab with all of the standard design choices for a chart.

On the far left side is the Add Chart Element dropdown menu that lets you choose which elements to include on the chart such as axes, axis titles, chart title, data labels, etc.

Next to that are the Quick Layout options that combine various chart elements which can be useful if one is close to what you want.

After that is the Change Colors dropdown menu that uses color palettes that work for your presentation theme. So for mine, for example, it defaulted to shades of turquoise but there are some options in the Change Colors dropdown that use more greens than blues as well as some monochromatic choices.

Next to that is the Chart Styles section with different layouts for the chart that may work for you. (Again, I covered all of this in lots of detail in the Excel books, so if you really want to learn about working with charts in office programs, Excel is where you do that. There's even a specific book that's just for charts that's an extract from the intermediate Excel titles for each series.)

Finally, at the very end of that tab there is an option to change the chart type. Sometimes you may find that you don't want a bar chart but instead want a column chart or something like that. Easy enough to do. Just be careful when trying to move between non-compatible types of charts because that will not work well.

If those options don't give you enough control, then go to the Format tab. That will let you manually change the shape fill or shape outline for your chart elements. Click on the element first, and then make your formatting choice. (Honestly, you probably won't need to do this too often if you're working with a good theme, but it's there when needed.)

Edit Chart or Axes Titles

Most of your data labeling will happen in the Excel spreadsheet where you add your data, but that's not the case for things like your chart title or the titles of each axis. Those you have to manually input.

To do so, click on the text that reads "Chart Title" or "Axis Title" in the chart itself, use Ctrl + A to select all of the text that's currently there, and then type in your new text. Click away when done.

If you want to format that text in a way that it isn't already formatted, click there, Ctrl + A to select the text, and then use the Font section of the Home tab or the Text Fill dropdown menu in the WordArt Styles section of the Format tab. Either one will work.

Note that while you could get fancy with the formatting of a chart title and use WordArt Styles that have outlines and shadows and who knows what else, you probably shouldn't. It will likely interfere with the ability of your audience to read your text.

* * *

You can also double-click on your chart, or right-click and choose the Format Plot Area or similar Format X choice from the dropdown menu, to open the chart format task pane on the right-hand side of your workspace. That will include a variety of formatting options related to your chart. Use the first dropdown arrow to choose the type of formatting you want to do:

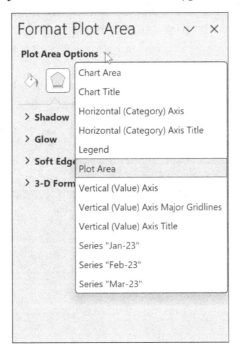

After that click through the various categories and options to find what you need.

Note that if you had a task pane open on the right-hand side already it may disappear and become an icon off to the side of this task pane. Like so:

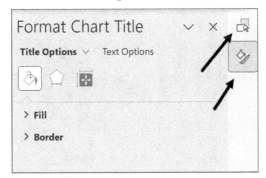

Here you can see that the Format Chart Title task pane is open but on the far right-hand side I have icons for that as well as the Selection task pane. If I click on that top icon it will switch over to the Selection task pane. If I click on the icon for Format Chart Title it will be hidden until I need it again.

Paste a Chart from Excel

Another option with PowerPoint is to build the chart in Microsoft Excel and then just treat it like a picture that you're copying from one program to another. Click on the chart in Excel, use Ctrl + C to copy, come back to PowerPoint, click on the slide where you want to paste the chart, and use Ctrl + V to paste.

When I just did that, the chart pasted in using the theme colors of my presentation in PowerPoint. I did have to click and drag from the corners to resize it to fit the space in the slide.

Also, when I chose to edit the data in that chart it opened the Excel file I had pulled the chart from. So don't copy an Excel chart from an Excel file unless that file will remain available in the same location or you have no intention of editing the chart.

Another option is to Paste Special - Picture. That will paste the chart in as a picture which means it will use the colors you used in Excel and you also won't be able to change anything on the chart at all.

Other Tips and Tricks

Rulers, Gridlines, and Guides

If you go to the Show section of the View tab there are checkboxes there for Ruler, Gridlines, and Guides.

Ruler will place a ruler along the top and left-hand side of your slide.

Guides by default will place dotted lines that run through the center point for the slide, so through the zero point on the ruler, although you can left-click and drag a guide line to a specific point on the ruler if you need to.

It's very hard to see, but here I have a line running across at the zero mark for the left-hand side, but I've moved the guideline for the top ruler over to 4. As you drag you'll see the value where the guideline is so you can know where you're lined up.

Having a guideline on your slide lets you manually position elements and make sure that they're aligned. This can allow you to keep positioning consistent across slides even when your elements are not left-aligned, right-aligned, or centered.

The final view option is to put gridlines over the entire slide that create one-inch by one-inch squares that you can also use for aligning elements:

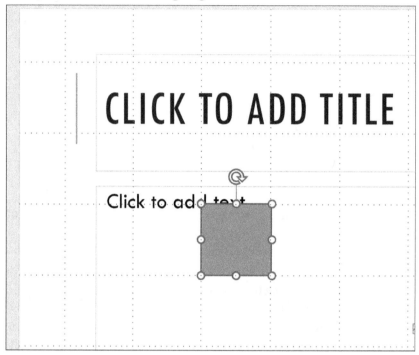

The grid is built from the center of the slide outward, so the rectangles along the edges are not fully one-inch square.

Neither guidelines nor gridlines will be visible on the presentation. They're just there for you to use as you prepare your document.

Equations

If you lecture using mathematical equations then the Symbols section of the Insert tab will provide a lot of help for you. Click on the dropdown menu for Equation to see some common equations such as the Area of a Circle. Or go to the bottom of the dropdown and click on Insert New Equation or Ink Equation.

Insert New Equation will open an Equation tab for you that has all of the elements of an equation. Click on them to build your equation. Use the Structures section for some common structures such as a fraction. The boxes for each equation component can then be clicked on to add specific values like x, y, a number or another equation component.

Ink Equation lets you write your math into a field and then PowerPoint will convert that to an equation for you. This probably works best if you have a stylus, but it just managed to decipher my very poorly-done writing of 2+2 using my mouse.

Esc to exit if you need to.

WordArt

We have briefly seen the WordArt option more than once as we've been walking through the various elements you can insert into a slide. WordArt can also be found in the Text section of the Insert tab. Click on the dropdown arrow there to see various formatting choices that are pre-populated.

If you click on one of those options, PowerPoint will insert a text box that says, "Your text here" with text that is formatted that way. It will also bring up a Shape Format tab that has the WordArt Styles section:

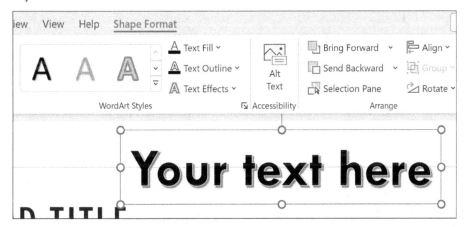

In addition to the twenty pre-formatted options available in that section, you can change the Text Fill color and the Text Outline color to anything you want. In the Text Effects dropdown menu you can choose Shadow, Reflection, Glow, Bevel, 3-D Rotation, or Transform options.

I do know a few people who have used PowerPoint over the years to design book covers. In those instances, these settings can be very useful. So I'm mentioning them, but not focusing on them, because in a basic business presentation, WordArt should be used sparingly or not at all.

Other Text Formatting

I covered most text formatting options in the first book in this series, but there were a few I left out. Three are available in the Font section of the Home tab:

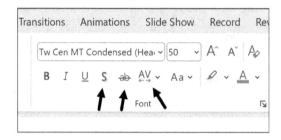

The first one there, that looks like a blurry S is text shadowing which will put a shadow behind your text.

The next one, which looks like an a and a b with a line through them is strikethrough which will put a strikethrough across a line of text.

The third one there in that bottom row is character spacing and it has a dropdown menu because there are choices for very tight, tight, normal, loose, and very loose.

Here are examples of all three of the above:

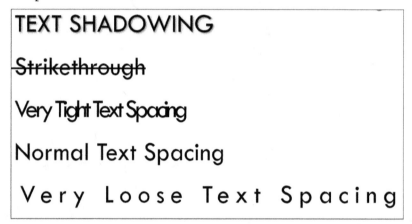

There are also a few additional options in the Font dialogue box. Select your text and then click on the expansion arrow in the bottom right corner of the Font section of the Home tab, or right-click and choose Font from the dropdown menu to see that dialogue box.

The additional choices available here are Double Strikethrough, Superscript, Subscript, Small Caps, and All Caps.

Symbols

If you ever need to insert a symbol into your presentation, you can do so using the Symbol option in the Symbols section of the Insert tab. Click on that to open the Symbol dialogue box. Find the symbol you want and double-click on it or click on it once and then click on Insert at the bottom of the dialogue box.

The Symbol dialogue box will stay open after it inserts your symbol for you. Click on the X in the top right corner to close it when you're done.

Symbols can be formatted with colors, font size, etc. just like text.

Format Slide Background

If you're working with a presentation theme, chances are you won't need to do this, but if you ever do need to change the background color on a slide or series of slides, go to the Customize section of the Design tab and click on Format Background.

This will open the Format Background task pane where you can then choose from a solid fill, gradient fill, picture or texture fill, or pattern fill. You can also choose a color and a degree of transparency. This will fill the entire slide but behind any elements on that slide.

Here, for example, I added a striped background to this slide but it only shows in the space behind the photo:

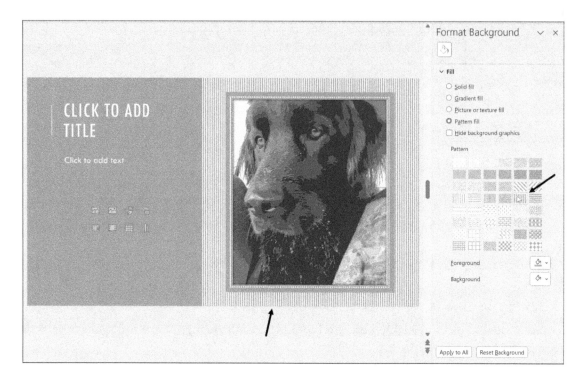

Format Background or Perimeter of Text Box

You can also change the background in a text box by right-clicking on that element and choosing the Format Shape option. It will open the Format Shape task pane where you have choices for solid fill, etc. as well as no fill for that text box. If you choose an option other than no fill there will be options for color and transparency as well.

This is also where you can add a solid-colored or gradient line around the perimeter of the text box using the options under Line.

Import From Word

It is possible to write an outline in Word that you then import into PowerPoint where each new section of the outline becomes a new slide and then the subpoints of the outline are the bullet points on the slide. To make it work, you need to use the Heading styles for each level of your outline when you create it in Word.

Once you have the outline, save it, and then go to the Slides section of the Home tab in PowerPoint, click on the dropdown under New Slide, and choose Slides from Outline. Navigate to where you saved the Word file and choose it. PowerPoint will then convert that outline into a presentation for you.

Select All

To select all of the objects on a page or all of the text in a text box use Ctrl + A. What is actually selected will depend on where your cursor was or was not at the time you used the shortcut. If text is selected it will be shaded gray. If elements are selected you'll see white circles around their edges. You can also click into the slides task pane and select all the slides there using Ctrl + A.

There is also a Select dropdown available in the Editing section of the Home tab which has options for Select All, Select Objects, and Selection Pane.

Slide Transitions

In the last book we discussed how to have different elements on a slide appear at different times. There are also options for creating special transitions between slides.

I have seen this used very effectively, but most of the time it is not, so exercise caution.

Click on the thumbnail of the slide you want to transition *to* in the left-hand task pane, go to the Transitions tab, and then click on the transition type you want to use from the Transition To This Slide set of options.

You can use the Preview option in the Transitions tab to see what the transition will look like.

To control how long the transition takes, adjust the value in the Timing section of the Transitions tab. You can also control if the transition requires a mouse click or is set to automatically happen after a set period of time from that section. And if there's a sound that should play at the same time.

The one time I saw this very effectively used was in a presentation that was running before a talk on prisoner abuse where the presentation had been set up to move from one image of prisoner abuse to another every five seconds or so. I think it was also paired with a ticking sound. It really made those images hit home and set the stage for the talk (which was about the psychology of evil). So this can be done well and does have uses. Just maybe be careful about using it in a normal business presentation just to have each slide appear in a different way.

Master Slides

I consider master slides an advanced-level topic, because changes made to master slides impact all of the slides in a presentation and so messing around in there is a very good way to screw it all up real fast.

But I started at a new employer recently and someone had really messed things up in the corporate template. As in, I couldn't make a multi-level bulleted list no matter what I did. Because this person had gone into the master slide and limited it to one bullet level. I don't think they meant to, but that's what they did.

So I want to at least let you know where to look if you run into this sort of issue.

You can see your master slides by going to the View tab and clicking on Slide Master under Master Views. Here's the first few master slides for the theme I've been using throughout this book:

Any change to that top slide will impact all of the other master slides in the theme as well as every single slide in the presentation. A change to one of the other slides below that will just impact slides that use that layout.

Here's what a master slide looks like:

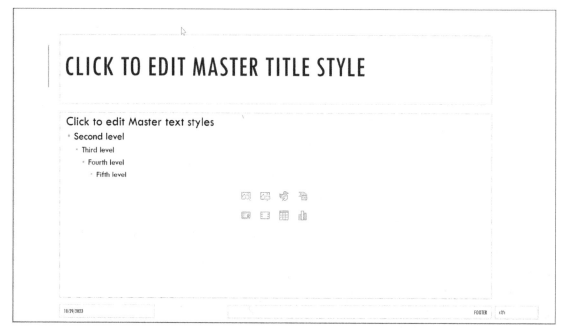

See that list of bulleted items there that goes down to a fifth level? If you want to have a five-level bulleted list, it needs to show that way in the master slide. That's the issue I had at my new employer. Whoever built the template stopped at the first-level bullet.

You can edit a master slide to change the appearance of your slides.

So, say for example, I don't like that the first level of text in this slide has no bullet. I could go into the top master slide and change that.

But I really would recommend exercising caution here. Because that change will impact every single slide in the presentation. Perhaps in a negative way.

In my opinion, the best thing to do is choose a good presentation theme up front that has addressed all of this and then just live with the choices they made when they created it.

But in case you need it, that's where you find it. Just maybe save a backup copy first before you start mucking around in there?

To exit the master slide view, click on Close Master View in the top menu.

Sections

If you have a really long presentation, consider inserting sections into the presentation. When you have sections you can then collapse them so that it's easier to navigate through the slides in the left-hand side of your workspace. You can also click and drag to move an entire section at once if needed and can print that section of slides easily.

To create a new section, right-click onto the space in the left-hand navigation pane that is directly above the slide that you want to have start your new section. So not on the slide itself, but in the gray space around it. Choose Add Section from the dropdown menu:

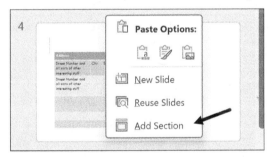

A Rename Section dialogue box will pop up and let you name the section. Type in the name you want and then click on Rename.

If you add sections, you sort of need to commit to using them throughout the presentation, because all slides from that point forward will be assigned to that section.

Once you've inserted a section, you can click on the arrow to the left of the section name to collapse the section and hide all slides in that section. If it's already collapsed, click there to expand it.

Here I've created four sections and you can see that for the three sections at the top that are collapsed (Default Section, Tables, and Picture Videos SmartArt) it shows the number of slides in each section. For the section that is not collapsed, Charts, it just shows the slides:

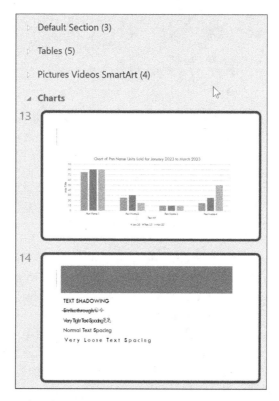

To rename or remove a section later, right-click on the section name:

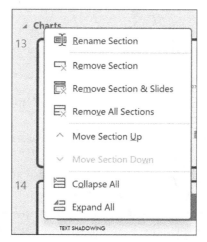

You can choose to rename the section, remove the section, remove all sections, or remove that section as well as its slides. There are also options in that dropdown to collapse or expand all sections at once.

To move a section, either use the Move Section Up or Move Section Down options in that dropdown, or left-click the section name and drag until the section is where you want it. When you move a section that will move all slides in that section as well.

It is possible to include a link to a section of slides from another slide. Click and drag the section name onto that slide. That will let you jump in your presentation to that set of slides before you then come back to the original slide and continue on with your presentation.

When you do this, it will embed a small image of the first slide in the section onto that other slide. When presenting, just click on that image and it will make it full-size and then let you move through the slides of that section before once more minimizing the image and returning to the first slide.

Comments

PowerPoint doesn't have a track changes function like Word does. The next best option is to use Comments rather than do something like [have we verified this number] in the middle of the text on a slide. Typing text that should not be there onto a slide is a good way to embarrass yourself when it comes time to present.

So use comments if you have something to say when reviewing a presentation.

To insert a comment, click onto that point in the presentation and then go to the Review tab and click on New Comment. That will open the Comments task pane on the right-hand side of the workspace:

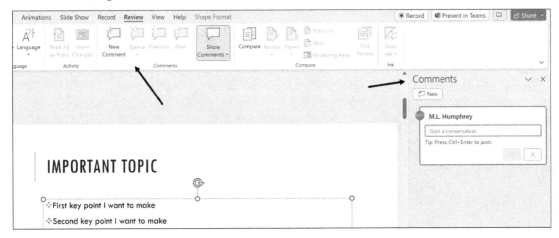

In the "start a conversation" field, type whatever you want to say. Use Ctrl + Enter to finalize the comment or click on the bright orangeish arrow.

Below each comment that's added, there will be a Reply field. Click into that to add any response to the original comment. You can also just click on the little thumbs up sign to like someone else's comment.

Click on the three dots on the right-hand side of the comment for options to delete the thread or mark it as resolved. Here we have one comment with a response, the next one with a thumbs up, and you can see the options to delete or resolve that comment:

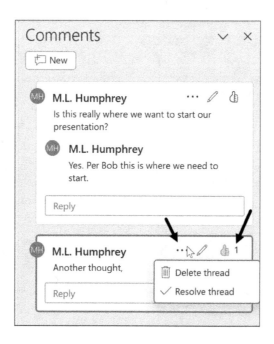

Comments do not show on the presentation itself. But if there are comments and you click on that slide they will appear in the Comment task pane.

If you want a note on the slide itself, choose the Show Comments dropdown in the Comments section of the Review tab and select Show Advanced Markup.

You can also use the Comments section of the Review tab to navigate to the previous or next comment. The Delete option in that section allows you to delete that one comment, delete all comments on the slide, or delete all comments in the presentation.

Save As Other Formats

I already covered in the introductory book in this series the basics of saving a PowerPoint file, but now I want to cover two special cases, saving as a PDF and saving as an image.

As a reminder, to save a file as a different format you need to go to the File tab and click on Save As. There is a dropdown menu on that Save As screen that will then let you choose the file format you want:

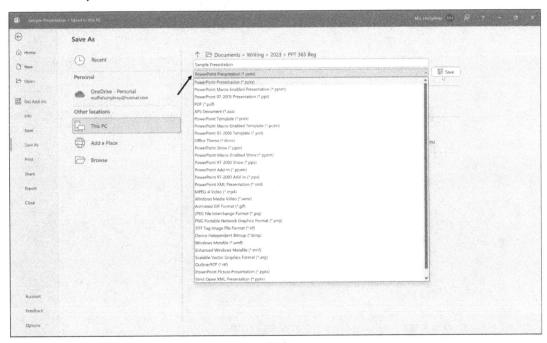

PDF

Depending on your available programs, you may actually have a Save as PDF option on the left-hand side that you can click on if you want a PDF file. That saves a step and will immediately bring up a dialogue box where you can choose your location and file name.

But for us mere mortals without that fancy set-up, click on Save As, and then in the dropdown menu for format choose PDF from the list. For me right now it's the fourth one down.

When I chose that, PowerPoint brought up an option about investigating accessibility. I am going to ignore it for now. We'll cover accessibility in a moment.

If you like the name for the document and the current location, just click on Save. If not, click into the name field and change it or click on Browse to navigate to a new location for the file.

You could have also started with the Browse option and changed the Save As Type in the dropdown menu in that Save As dialogue box to PDF. That's another way to do it.

Either way, click Save when you have the name, location, and file type set. Your PowerPoint will save with default settings, which means one slide per page and just the slide.

If you want more control over what you are turning into a PDF, click on Browse to bring up the Save As dialogue box, change the type to PDF, and then click on Options in the bottom section of the dialogue box to open the Options dialogue box:

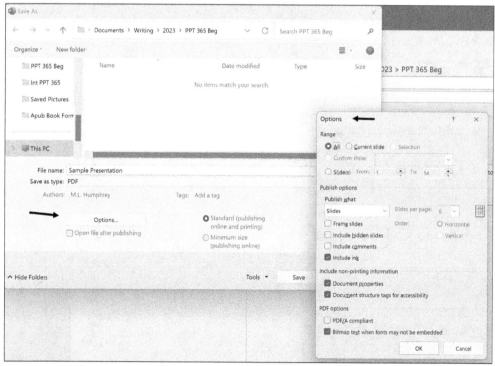

Let's just walk down your options from top to bottom.

First up, you can choose to print all slides, the current slide, a selection of slides (but you have to do that before you choose to print), or a range of slides (but you have to know before you choose to print what the slide range you want is).

For non-continuous slides, so say slides 4, 10, and 12, you'd use selection and hold down the Ctrl key as you clicked on each one you wanted in the main workspace before coming to Save As.

Next, you can choose to print the slides which will put each slide in your presentation on one page in landscape format. Your other options there are to print handouts, note pages, or an outline view, just like we discussed in the introductory book of this series for printing. You can also set here the number of slides to print per page.

Keep in mind this will be "printed" to a PDF file.

Next there are checkboxes to add a frame around your slides, to include any hidden slides from the presentation, to include comments added to any slide, and to include ink that was added to the slide.

After that you can choose whether to include the document properties and any document structure tags for accessibility.

Essentially all of those are print settings but applied to saving your PDF.

Finally, you can choose whether to make your PDF compliant with the PDF/A standard and whether to turn fonts that can't be embedded into the presentation into bitmap text. If you're just printing your slides as handouts, don't worry about these last two at all. That is more for when you need the PDF to upload somewhere, like a publication site.

* * *

Another option for creating a PDF is to go to File and then use the Export option instead and choose Create PDF/XPS Document. That will bring up a Publish as PDF or XPS dialogue box. Just make sure your Save As type is PDF. It should be by default.

(As a side note, I once had an analyst turn documents into XPS files instead of PDF and the recipient of those files lost their mind over it, so only use XPS if it's for you or you have already confirmed with the other party that they can handle XPS files. That was not a fun afternoon for me.)

Image Files

Early on when I was writing the first versions of these books and I needed images that had labels on them, I used PowerPoint to do that. I took my screenshot, dropped the image into a slide on PowerPoint and then added arrows and text boxes to label what needed labeled.

In order to be able to then use that in a book I had to export the slides as images. Not the best or easiest way to do that, but it worked. So if you ever need something similar or have another reason for turning your slides into image files, you can do that.

To do so, go to File, Save As, and choose the type of image file you want from the Save As Type dropdown.

The most common type of image files people want is usually JPEG File Interchange Format (.jpg) or PNG Portable Network Graphics Format (.png).

If you're doing something like this book, though, use TIFF Tag Image File Format (.tif) instead. Don't ask me why now, but I went down a very long rabbit hole over this and ultimately something about lossless compression and image integrity blah, blah, blah led me to decide that for the non-fiction books I publish .tif is the best format. Probably more because of the ebooks than the print books, though.

Anyway. Make your choice and click on Save.

PowerPoint is then going to bring up a dialogue box that asks "Which Slides Do You Want to Export?" and give you the choice between All Slides and Just This One. You can also choose Cancel.

The way this works is that PowerPoint will take each individual slide and turn it into an image for you. So if you choose All Slides and you have a hundred slides in that presentation, it will create a hundred image files for you. They will all be saved into a folder that uses the presentation name. Like so:

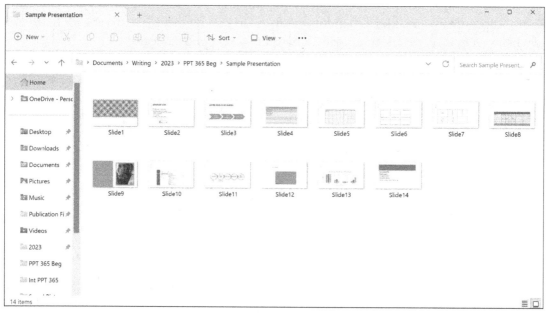

See how each image of a slide is named Slide 1, Slide 2, etc. based on the order in the presentation.

Even if you try to select just a subset of slides, your choices will still only be All or One.

If you choose to save just one slide instead, PowerPoint will save that one slide as an image using the name you provided in the Save As screen. Remember it is only that one image, not all of them. So even if it has a name like "Sample Presentation", it will still just be an image of that one slide.

(Maybe that's obvious to you, but the first time I tried this it was not in fact obvious to me.)

GIF

You can use the animated gif choice in the dropdown to create a little animation of your entire presentation that will walk through from start to finish with all of your transitions and videos, etc. But if you're going to use this option, you really should review the timing of the various transitions in your slide to make sure it's slow enough for people to follow. By default mine really was not.

Accessibility

PowerPoint now has a lot of accessibility tools built in that you can use. It will tell you when you don't have alternative text on an image or when a color choice isn't going to work for all members of an audience.

To see the accessibility choices, go to the Accessibility section of the Review tab. There is a dropdown menu there for Check Accessibility that has a number of options: Check Accessibility, Alt Text, Reading Order Pane, etc:

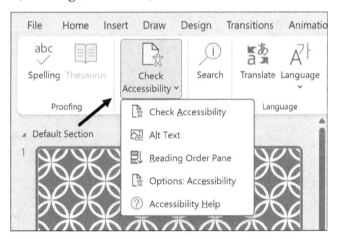

Click on Check Accessibility to see the Accessibility task pane with various suggestions:

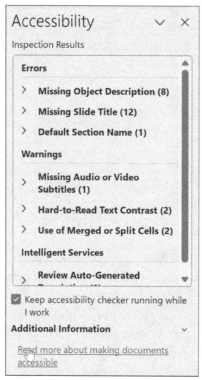

You can click on the arrow for each one to expand it and see where the error is and then click on that item to go to that point in the presentation. PowerPoint will also explain to you what the issue is. So here it says that the contrast between my white text and that turquoise background may be hard to read:

I don't necessarily agree. But if I did, when I click on that item it also shows me the Change Colors option so that I can immediately go and fix that without having to search around for how to do so.

The bigger your audience, probably the more you should pay attention to these alerts. Especially pay attention to errors related to color blindness for a visual presentation because about 8% of men have some form of color blindness.

For presentations that you're going to post online for someone to read through, then alt text becomes more important for your images.

Anyway. Something to consider to reach a wider audience with your presentation. You can also click on the Accessibility: Investigate option at the bottom left of your workspace to open that task pane if you don't want to go to the Accessibility tab.

Conclusion

Alright. That's it for this book. There are still things you can do in PowerPoint that we did not cover, but at this point you should be perfectly capable of putting together a nice, solid PowerPoint presentation that incorporates images, videos, SmartArt, etc.

Of course, the world is unpredictable so who knows what will come up in the future that you need to know. Good news is that Microsoft has very good help available.

If there's something specific that you want to know about, often the easiest way to learn more is to hold your mouse over that option and see if there is a Tell Me More choice:

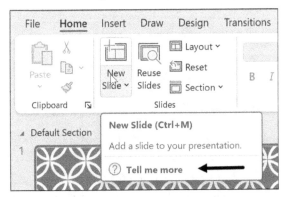

Click on that if there is. It will open the Help task pane on the right-hand side of the workspace to provide help for that specific topic:

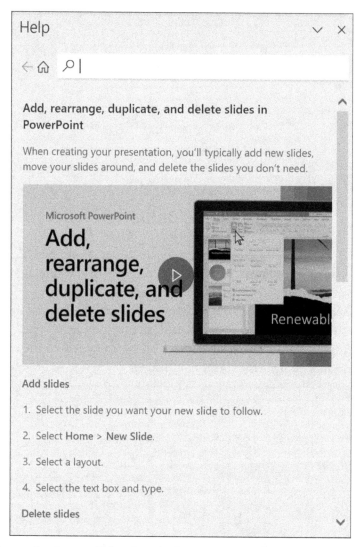

Depending on the topic, there will be descriptive text or maybe a video like in this case.

If there isn't a Tell Me More option to click on, you can also just go to the Help tab and click on Help there to open the task pane and then search for the topic you want to know more about.

If you just want general training, the Show Training option under the Help tab will bring up various topics that you can click on to see more information.

If all else fails, search the internet. I like to search using "PowerPoint 365" and then the topic I'm interested in. I try to look for the microsoft support results.

One final note, under that Help tab there is a What's New option. Click on that to get the New Features and Updates link in the right-hand task pane. This will let you see recent changes to PowerPoint 365 as well as upcoming changes.

If you're going to use 365 programs you have to accept that they may change on you without much control on your end. On one hand, that's great, you always have the latest and greatest. On another hand it sucks, because you get used to how something works and then maybe you walk in one day and it's all different. (Or you're writing a book on PowerPoint and someone just randomly decides to change the default options in the text box of a slide without notice, making your book instantly out of date.)

And the changes aren't in my opinion as fully vetted as when they do a big formal new product release. I just clicked on that link and there were changes made on September 28, October 10, October 25, and October 31. The changes to PowerPoint were mostly error fixes, but when you're updating things on a rolling, ongoing basis like that sometimes bad things slip through. Or you get something that's half-baked and they want users to give them free feedback to finalize it.

So 365 programs are probably going to be a little more buggy than working in a fixed version, like PowerPoint 2019, but the fixes that are needed will probably happen faster. Which is why knowing how to use Help and checking for what's new are both good skills to have when working in 365.

Okay. Real quick. What didn't we cover that you may still need to know?

I didn't cover working in Teams, so if you are in an organization that uses Teams, you may want to explore how that works. I also didn't cover how to Record a presentation. If you need that, check out the Record tab. I didn't go into full detail about the accessibility options. I didn't cover the various View choices you have. Nor did I cover Macros or Drawing tools.

That's because these books are geared towards the average user who has average needs. You may need more. But hopefully you now have that solid foundation to work from so that it's easy to go and find what you need.

If you get stuck, feel free to reach out. I don't check my email daily, but I do check it and will help if I can. Some of the items I didn't cover are because in twenty-five years I've never needed them but I'm happy to find help resources for you if you can't find them or try it myself and see what issues I run into.

Finally, I've said this before but I want to say it again: Always keep in mind what your goal is with your presentation. Don't add bells and whistles unless they support that goal. And remember that the more you put on a slide in terms of text, the less your audience is going to be paying attention to you. That's just human nature.

Alright, then. Good luck with it.

Index

About the Author

M.L. Humphrey is a former stockbroker with a degree in Economics from Stanford and an MBA from Wharton who has spent close to twenty years as a regulator and consultant in the financial services industry.

You can reach M.L. at mlhumphreywriter@gmail.com or at mlhumphrey.com.